YALE SCHOOL OF ARCHITECTURE

YALE SCHOOL OF ARCHITECTURE

EDWARD P. BASS DISTINGUISHED
VISITING ARCHITECTURE FELLOWSHIP

POETRY, PROPERTY, AND PLACE 01:

STEFAN BEHNISCH / GERALD HINES

Nina Rappaport, editor
with Markus Dochantschi and Jonah Gamblin

Yale School of Architecture
180 York Street
New Haven, Connecticut 06520
www.architecture.yale.edu

Distributed by
W. W. Norton & Company, Inc.
500 Fifth Avenue
New York, NY 10110
www.wwnorton.com

This book was made possible through The Edward P. Bass Distinguished Visiting Architecture Fellowship Fund of the Yale School of Architecture. It is the first in a series of publications of the Bass Fellowship published through the Dean's office.

Edited by Nina Rappaport, Markus Dochantschi and Jonah Gamblin

Design: mgmt. design, Brooklyn, NY.

Cover: Image from Bass Fellowship Studio, Ceren Bingol, 2006.

Library of Congress Cataloging-in-Publication Data

Poetry, property, and place : Stefan Behnisch, Gerald Hines / Nina Rappaport, editor ; Markus Dochantschi and Jonah Gamblin, assistant editors. – 1st ed.

p. cm. – (The Edward P. Bass Distinguished Visiting Architecture Fellowship ; 1)

ISBN-13: 978-0-393-73220-7 (pbk.)
ISBN-10: 0-393-73220-7 (pbk.)

1. Architects and builders. 2. Behnisch, Stefan–Interviews.
3. Hines, Gerald D.–Interviews. 4. Architecture–Study and teaching–Connecticut–New Haven. I. Behnisch, Stefan. II. Hines, Gerald D. III. Rappaport, Nina. IV. Dochantschi, Markus, 1968- V. Gamblin, Jonah. VI. Series: Edward P. Bass Distinguished Visiting Architecture Fellowship (Series) ; 1.

NA2543.B84P64 2006
720–dc22

2006010501

CONTENTS

I. THE VALUE OF DESIGN: ARCHITECTS AND DEVELOPERS

II. GARIBALDI REPUBBLICA AND THE FOUNDATION OF FASHION MILAN (MODAM)

III. MODAM AT YALE: THE BEHNISCH-HINES STUDIO

Preface: Nina Rappaport, Markus Dochantschi, and Jonah Gamblin This book—*Poetry, Property, and Place*, the first in a series—documents the Edward P. Bass Distinguished Visiting Architecture Fellowship at the Yale School of Architecture for which Gerald Hines, Bass Fellow, and Stefan Behnisch, Saarinen Visiting Professor, led an advanced studio in the spring semester of 2005 that explored with students the approach to the design and economic development of a public place with a cultural building in the heart of Milan.

The project for a Museum of Fashion and Design (MOdAM) on the piazza Garibaldi Repubblica, a major project currently being redeveloped by the Hines organization, served as the program and site for the students' design investigations. Following an introduction by Dean Robert A. M. Stern explaining the premise behind the establishment of the Bass Fellowship, the book is organized into three sections: The first section, "Architect and Developer," features interviews with Stefan Behnisch and Gerald Hines, as well as the studio brief and the analyses the students formulated. The second section, "Garibaldi Repubblica and the Foundation of Fashion Milan," includes interviews with Gianni Verga, Councilor for Land Development, Milan City Council, and Beatrice Trussardi, CEO of Trussardi (a sponsor of the Foundation for Fashion), each discussing the project in terms of the evolving role of fashion in the economy and culture of Milan. This section also presents the operative Master Plan by Pelli Clarke Pelli, commissioned by Hines, in which the Yale students were asked to set their specific proposals. The third section, "MOdAM at Yale," features the students' designs organized thematically: programming and organization; public space; circulation and infrastructure; surface, fashion, and performance enclosure; and style and iconic form. The descriptive commentary on selected student projects includes discussion by the students, as well as responses from the panel of architects and developers at the midterm and final reviews. The book concludes with excerpts from the summary discussion that took place at the end of the final reviews on April 29, 2005.

The writing, editing, and design of a book parallels that of the building process, as ideas are assembled and organized to illuminate a project. The editors would like to acknowledge the work of the students who participated in the studio and who were instrumental in realizing this book's publication: Benjamin Albertson, Forth Bagley, Garo Balmanoukian, Ceren Bingol, Marissa Brown, Genevieve Fu,

Jonah Gamblin, Jennifer Newsom, J. Fiona Ragheb, and Brett Spearman. We would also like to thank those who participated in interviews and to staff in various offices who assisted with images, including those of Stefan Behnisch, Gerald Hines, Cesar Pelli, Gianni Verga, and Beatrice Trussardi. We would also like to thank the graphic designers, Sarah Gephart and Rachel Griffin of mgmt. design in New York; David Delp, copy editor; Nancy Green of W. W. Norton Books, our distributor; and Dean Robert A. M. Stern for guiding the process.

Poetry, Property, and Place: Dean Robert A. M. Stern The Edward P. Bass Distinguished Visiting Architecture Fellowship, inaugurated in 2005, was the result of an endowment from Mr. Bass ('67 BA, '72 March). The Bass Fellowship brings property developers to the Yale School of Architecture on a regular basis as visiting fellows, each participating throughout the course of a semester as an integral member of an advanced design studio or seminar led by senior design faculty or those occupying visiting professorships at the school. To this end, the design studio or seminar in which the Bass Fellow participates is organized around a development project with which the fellow is currently engaged and may incorporate the participation of other members of the fellow's project development team.

A few words about Ed Bass. After leaving the Yale School of Architecture, Bass embarked on a dual career as environmentalist and city builder, sponsoring the Biosphere 2 development thirty miles north of Tucson, Arizona, and undertaking the downtown revitalization of his home city, Fort Worth, Texas, where his Sundance Square Development combined the restoration and renovation of derelict historic properties with the construction of sympathetically designed new ones, transforming the nearly dead core into a vibrant, round-the-clock center that balanced office buildings, hotels, apartment houses, retail, entertainment, and performance venues. In taking on both the Biosphere and Fort Worth projects, Bass worked from the premise that is central to this school: Architecture is a socially grounded discipline, placing the art of building at the service of grand visions and everyday realities. The Yale School of Architecture sets high value on the artistic accomplishments of those who boldly and directly interact with the world around them.

The Bass Fellowship does not exist in a vacuum but is part of a larger discourse within the School of Architecture that includes courses in the economics and politics of large-scale urbanism and, at a small scale, studio experience that encounters the design and construction of artistically ambitious but modest-sized community structures as part of the First-Year Building Project, which every beginning architecture student in the school has participated in since 1967. The Building Project began with structures for remote towns in Appalachia, but since 1989 it has been focused each year on working with a community-based client for the rebuilding of New Haven's residential neighborhoods. Most recently, students worked with Neighborhood Housing Services (which sets the goals and actively participates in the design process).

When the gift of the fellowship was first announced, some seemed skeptical, as if the fox were being led into the henhouse. But leading American architects have worked in close and mutually respectful collaboration with developers for a very long time. It can be argued that many of American's greatest contributions to architecture have been the product of such collaborations: think of skyscrapers, of urban ensembles like Grand Central's Terminal City or Rockefeller Center. Ever since William Zeckendorf assembled his own in-house architectural team led by I. M. Pei, who in turn had on his staff architects Harry Cobb, Ulrich Franzen, and James Stewart Polshek, top developers have regularly made it their business to seek out top architectural talent. Given that Cobb, Franzen, and Polshek were also active as design critics at Yale, the spadework for the Bass initiative can be said to have first begun in New Haven a generation ago. When Pei went to work for Zeckendorf, he was criticized for mixing high-minded aesthetics with base economics. As Pei's contemporaries were wont to put it: "One cannot run with the hare and hunt with the hounds." The precedent of a collegial relationship between architects and developers is not confined to the world of New York real-estate, but can also be seen in the early American work of Mies van der Rohe, many of whose most important buildings in Chicago were commissioned by the developer Herbert Greenwald. And many of today's leading architects, who are now making their mark with cultural projects where results are not measured by specific returns on investments, still maintain very strong ties to commercial developers. In this regard, one thinks of Frank Gehry and the Rouse Company, the Related Companies, and Forest City Ratner.

The Bass Fellowship is a welcome antidote to the tendency found in too many schools of architecture to frame the discussion of design largely, even exclusively, around the architect's point of view, with little acknowledgment of or participation by the many others who contribute to the building process: consulting engineers, city officials, and especially clients, who increasingly are not private patrons or even public officials but property developers. To infantilize the design process by never introducing the user or the client into the classroom or studio is naïve and self-destructive. Imagine a medical school where would-be doctors never encountered living patients or listened to their concerns! By introducing the student architect to the dialogue between master developer and master design architect, the Bass Fellowship helps ensure that beginning architects see their work in relationship to the social and economic forces of the marketplace.

In Spring 2005, Gerald D. Hines was the inaugural Bass Fellow. The choice of Mr. Hines and his willingness to accept the appointment reflects the leadership he has shown over the years in recognizing the value that excellent architecture and excellent architects can bring to the development process. As founder and director of Hines Interests Limited Partnership, an international development powerhouse with some of the world's most important large-scale urban projects in its purview, Gerald Hines has been working as a developer for fifty years. His strong interest in design is evident in his selection of leading design architects like Philip Johnson, Bruce Graham, Kevin Roche, Cesar Pelli, and Norman Foster to shape his buildings. Hines began his career in Houston, Texas, in the 1950s when the city was experiencing explosive growth. Hines not only developed some of the city's biggest buildings with the participation of leading architects, he made his buildings the most talked-about development projects of their time. Hines recognized that architects could bring more value to the relatively formulaic office building not only by making better-looking buildings, but also by helping to think through the relationship of buildings to their urban settings. Although office buildings are the bread-and-butter of the Hines portfolio, the firm has also undertaken complex, groundbreaking mixed-use projects such as the Houston Galleria, with its combination of department stores, shops, hotels, office buildings, as well as restaurants, movie theaters, and an ice-skating rink.

Stefan Behnisch, Eero Saarinen Visiting Professor of Architecture, collaborated with Hines in the Yale studio. With his architectural practice both in Stuttgart, Germany, and Venice, California, Behnisch has earned a reputation for artistically challenging, environmentally sophisticated buildings. He has designed the headquarters for the Deutsche Bank in Frankfurt and has new projects under development in Moscow, Russia, where, he says, the process is very different from that of his native Germany and the United States. Although most of Behnisch's work has been awarded through the public competition process that is typical in Germany and other European countries, his first American building was the headquarters for the biotech firm Genzyme in Cambridge, Massachusetts, which was a developer's project.

Gerald Hines proposed the studio topic Garibaldi Repubblica, a neglected site in the heart of Milan being developed under guidelines proposed in the Master Plan by Pelli Clark Pelli. The site was devastated in a bombing in World War II and until the Hines organization took it on, defied governmental efforts to harness its potential. The assumption of the studio was that the real challenge before the developer is not the realization of the commercial properties (office buildings and hotels) but the design of the cultural centerpiece that would be the project's signature attraction and a new magnet for the center of Milan. Significantly, as in so much institutional development today, that centerpiece—the Museum of Fashion and Design (MOdAM)—would be constructed by the developer. Because MOdAM was still being conceptualized in anticipation of a design competition, it was Hines' expectation that the students would bring new ideas to the project at a decisive moment in its formation. Despite the assignment that focused specifically on a building and not the master plan, some students chose to offer their own master planning proposals, which were presented at the mid-review when Cesar Pelli found himself confronted, in the presence of his client, with alternate arrangements for the site. While Hines and Jay Wyper, managing director of Hines Europe, said that the master plan ideas were too late to adopt because crucial decisions had already been made, who knows what conversations have since taken place in the Hines office about these student ideas?

The dialogue among Behnisch, assistant teacher Markus Dochantschi (who for seven years was a close collaborator Zaha Hadid's), Gerald Hines, and Jay Wyper (who was trained as an architect before becoming a developer) let students witness architects and developers in side-by-side collaboration. The students were surprised to see that developers talked in the same way that the students thought only architects talked about the secrets of good building and urban design; the developers were not interested just in dollars per square foot and return on their investments.

What has the inaugural Bass Fellowship studio taught us? For one thing, it has made clear that the developer doesn't always have different goals from the architect; that, in fact, the developer might be even more sensitive to the quality of public space than the architect, who is sometimes overly object-fixated. It has taught us that among talented and intelligent people in different but related fields, there can be mutual respect and a true exchange of ideas. In fact, as Ed Bass assumed when he endowed this fellowship, developers have a lot to teach students who many feared would be indifferent. The Bass Fellowship puts to rest the notion that the developer is some kind of nineteenth-century monopolist who operates outside the community. Certainly, developers such as those that the Bass Fellowship is expected to attract to Yale are ones who work with the best architects and urban strategists, as well as with the complex mix of interests and people of local communities.

The design discussion presented in this book makes clear that the developer's focus on architecture is much deeper than a simple preoccupation with the bottom line. The collaboration between Hines and Behnisch demonstrates that the relationship to a larger sphere of social values is essential to the economic success of a project. The studio juxtaposed the reciprocal worlds of architect and developer to posit fundamental questions: Should architects be more concerned with profitability and the developer more concerned with design? Where do the two meet? Should these priorities be reconciled? It led the students to envision increased collaboration, essential in today's political and economic environment. By explicitly linking a cultural project to the economy of the city, it became clear that the work of an architect, no matter the programmatic brief, necessarily must consider demographics, circulation, transportation, quantified analysis, planning options—and the bottom line. Moreover, it made plain that the startling originality of singular buildings was not enough in itself; indeed, public space is a crucial component of artistic excellence. In short, this interdisciplinary collaboration was a triple threat, combining sophisticated environmentalism, responsible urban development, and the search for significant form.

I would like to extend my thanks to Edward Bass for the gift of this fellowship that allows Yale to embark on this long-term project that is bound to have an impact on the future practice of architecture. And I would like to thank Gerald Hines, Jay Wyper, Stefan Behnisch, and Markus Dochantschi for their dedication to the work and to the students in the studio for taking on the challenge. I would also like to thank all of those in Milan and at Yale who broadened the topic, as well as the book's editors, Nina Rappaport, Markus Dochantschi, and Jonah Gamblin, for their work in conceptualizing and realizing *Poetry, Property, and Place*, the first in a series documenting the work of the Edward P. Bass Visiting Fellows program at Yale.

I. THE VALU
OF DESIGN
ARCHITECTS
DEVELOPER

E THE VALU OF DESIGN: ARCHITECTS AND RS DEVELOPERS

Stefan Behnisch, Eero Saarinen Visiting Professor at Yale

Gerald D. Hines, Edward P. Bass Distinguished Visiting Architecture Fellow at Yale

The Architect: Stefan Behnisch In an interview that continued throughout the semester at the Yale School of Architecture, Stefan Behnisch, Saarinen Visiting Professor, discussed with Nina Rappaport his work, ideas about sustainability, and the studio at Yale.

NR: You consider sustainable architecture an integral aspect of building as well as essential to comfort. How would you define sustainability as more than just the idea of a "green" architecture, as a broader term about the world and how we can survive with what we have?

SB: Our office in the United States is sometimes identified as one focused on sustainable architecture. This is understandable since, from a distance, characteristics are seen in black and white. But we see ourselves as architects in a broader context. However, I do understand that since this topic of sustainability is rather new and interesting, one likes to focus on it. We take it very seriously, but consider it still as one discipline within all planning disciplines or, better, as one instrument within a well-balanced orchestra. Maybe today, since it's new, it is brass, but hopefully soon it will be one of the leading violins.

I can't define it, but I can explain it. Sustainability in Germany is *Nachhaltigkeit*, which comes from the field of forestry, meaning that you don't harvest more than what can grow. Sustainability is similar but more complex than what most people understand. Most people narrow it down to energy consumption—kilowatt hours per square meter per year. People like to talk about what they can grasp, and numbers are easy to verify. But qualities are more difficult; you can describe or feel them, but you can't really measure them except in terms of productivity and well-being. So people tend to stick to quantity. But sustainability, which is coming into the foreground of the architectural discussion, is about qualities and buildings that serve people in the best way.

NR: Is sustainability more of a holistic concept rather than just about individual buildings—about how we sustain a building and how it sustains us?

SB: We are talking about zillions of years of history of our planet, but we have only experienced a small part of it. And so far we have almost managed to ruin our planet. The question is not whether

The Developer: Gerald D. Hines In an ongoing interview with Gerald D. Hines while he was the inaugural Edward P. Bass Distinguished Visiting Architecture Fellow at the Yale School of Architecture, he discussed with Nina Rappaport the different roles of architects and developers, collaborations, sustainable development, his early projects as well as current large-scale projects in his firm's portfolio.

NR: When you step back and think about your career as a developer, do you see yourself going in a different direction now? Where are your current projects, and what are your development and overall interests today?

GH: I am concerned about how big American cities that grew up around the automobile can possibly be sustainable. So a direction for us is the development of large-scale, multi-use projects with work/live situations, because people are going to revolt against the two-hour commutes. For large-scale projects, there are just not many people who can raise the capital to build complete areas of cities. And the competition isn't as stiff. If you want to develop one building on one site in London, for example, there might be twenty-five firms in competition, but for larger sites there are few as qualified as we are.

NR: Projects such as the Diagonal Mar Development, an 84-acre waterfront site in Barcelona, and the site that housed the Renault plant outside of Paris come to mind. What is your approach to building something on the scale of a city within a city?

GH: In Barcelona, we bought the site in bankruptcy, effectively what they call "suspension of payments" in Spain. They had assembled about 2 million square feet for office space, but there wasn't a market for offices. We went back to the planning group, changed the design, and there was no connection from the proposed park to the sea, so we said we would like to create residential buildings, and they suggested creating the park perpendicular to the sea and running it straight through the site. I said, "Put the apartment buildings on the park." And they said "Sure, we'll do it." That is how it turned out with a large lake, a huge park, and we ended up with 1,500 residential units and a successful redevelopment.

the planet will survive but whether we will. If we keep maintaining our attitude, this planet will shake us off and forget about mankind at some point.

NR: Don't you think sustainability really is an environmental and a political issue?

SB: I think it is a humanistic issue, less a political issue. Mankind is a little experiment of the universe, and I want this experiment to go well. We can't do much for it, but we can contribute a little bit. I think it is an aesthetic and moral attitude. There was great selfishness in the 1980s and 1990s that said, "Let's just rip off the planet and get it over with." So I think it is a moral issue. The political attitudes are, after all, just a reaction of the people's behavior, at least in democracies.

NR: Where does this moral philosophy and humanism come from in your background and education?

SB: It comes from many sources. I went to a Steiner Waldorf school, known for humanistic education. My boys go there now, and my mother went there. But I also studied philosophy with the Jesuits. I am not Catholic, but I majored in philosophy and spent a year studying Immanuel Kant. So for me it is also about trying to understand how human beings act and how we perceive things. There is one approach of the Jesuits that I truly like. It says that even though good and evil are not absolute categories, the judgment for our acting is motivationally driven. Even if you lie, if the motivation is right, then the lie in itself is not an evil deed. And even if you are a true Christian or believer in any religion, you can be an evil person if you do things out of selfishness or the wrong motivation. We are thinking the same thing here. Sustainability is not a religion to me. Architecture is a sign of our cultural development, and right now sustainability should be part of architecture because it is a pressing issue in our cultural and scientific development. We should be aware of it, and it should show in our cultural production, in architecture, and in art, too.

We all know that today's oil prices are not just a little bump in the road. Oil is a limited resource. I am convinced that it can last a long time, and we need it for our societies. A family that is poor has to learn to manage its money; a company that has economic problems has to learn to manage its financial resources; a country that has limited resources has to learn to manage them. And buildings

In Paris, our site adjacent to Pinault's billion-dollar museum on the island, is the largest site under development in Europe. It will be a fantastic 10 million-square-foot mixed-use neighborhood with residential, office, retail, and what the French call "equipments," which are schools and social-service facilities. We are working in conjunction with the city and its master plan to lay out the infrastructure and allocate different pieces—sizes of buildings and the amount of open space. We are the largest shareholder in the consortium; the other two are French.

NR: Is this similar to your role in the plan of the Garibaldi Repubblica area in Milan, which has been awaiting development for more than forty years? How do you organize a project of this scale at the level of management, owner, full developer, or in partnership with a city? Does it differ from place to place?

GH: The Milan project is 2 million square feet on 56 acres. It is also mixed use, with office and residential space, as well as a fashion museum and design school. The city is developing their largest park as part of the site, as well as municipal buildings and Lombardy regional office buildings. We have acquired the options on the land and have 90 percent ownership, so we are both the developer and the primary owner. We have engaged Cesar Pelli to work on the master plan, and then the city and the public will review the project. The local Milan office team came up with the project; the London office decides how the project will be financed, what the concept is going to be, and how much retail and residential there will be. It is a collaboration between our London and Houston offices, where my older son, Jeff, is the chief financial officer.

NR: What made you choose this as your site for the Yale advanced studio, and what aspect of it are you assigning to the students?

GH: We thought it would be more interesting for a studio to design the fashion museum rather than the office component, so the students get a chance to take a first crack at this. The project itself will have some type of mini architectural competition.

NR: How do you weigh your own aesthetic preferences against the foreign locality? How can you confirm that a building that you like will be received?

Behnisch, Behnisch & Partner, Norddeutsche Landesbank, headquarters for the North German State Clearing Bank, Hannover, Germany, 2002.
Net Rentable Area: 40,000 square meters.

Ingenhoven Overdiek und Partner, Uptown München developed by Hines Germany, Munich, Germany, 2004. Net Rentable Area: 84,301 square meters.

use a significant part of our resources, so architects, engineers, and politicians are not dealing with a minor problem.

NR: Do you want to simplify society and live in a primitive hut?

SB: No, I am not an advocate of back-to-nature or a return to the Stone Age. Although I think Rousseau was a fantastic philosopher—he triggered the *Gartenstadt* and back-to-nature movements—I don't believe in his approach. I do think that our environment should be more in the public focus, and I also believe that sustainability is one of the new planning disciplines in architecture. Once we master the subject, it will be as much a part of planning and building as any other element. There have always been movements that in their time were far advanced and in the foreground. If you consider the Eiffel Tower, the structural temptation outweighed everything else. Even the Hancock Center in Chicago showed the structural elements in its façade. Now high-rise buildings are not a structural challenge anymore. Today, it is sustainability.

NR: Do you think about ways to bring sustainability into the foreground of your architecture and education?

SB: What I see in our office is that there is not one single competition or design that does not ask for the incorporation of green solutions. It is not easy to plan environmentally sound and sustainable buildings, but in general it is easy to appear to be taking care of the topic. Architects add some photovoltaic cells, engineers talk about ventilation chimneys, and everybody hopes the topic will soon go away. The art is to incorporate it. It is no miracle, no secret science. It is mostly common sense ... and a significant amount of work and effort.

If you add it on, technically it is a sorry excuse. People don't have problems implementing air-conditioning systems in buildings, and they think operable windows, shading devices, and daylighting enhancements are miracles. But those are easier to manage than lift systems, elevators, and escalators. It is just moving the focus away from thinking that the way we have done it for the last twenty years is good reason to do it again.

GH: That's the judgment that a developer pays for with his pocketbook. You have to feel how the people respond to a particular type of architecture. You do as much market research as you can with the major tenants, and you show them examples; in Paris, we had a mini competition between four architects, and we showed the different buildings around to the different prospective users, and we got their feedback. We try to build local teams of the nationality where we are, so that it is not Americans going in and saying, "What we did in New York, we are going to do in Paris." We don't do that. You have to be sensitive to that, but we took Norman Foster to Warsaw and that was a success.

NR: The design part of a project seems to be where you like to be involved. How do you keep up with what is going on and work with architects as part of the development process?

GH: I get a lot of pleasure being involved in the design process. I am a builder, not as much a financier. I started out as a mechanical engineer from Purdue University with a focus on building systems. I was involved with Texas Engineering, which was the first consulting engineering firm in Houston. Our first building was a 20,000-square-foot office/warehouse, and it was the best of its kind in Houston. I had a lot of fun doing it; we made money, and we got five new jobs. I learned how to work with architects so they could bring in outstanding design at a reasonable cost, which is the crux of Hines' philosophy.

NR: When you put together a team, how do you work with the architects and have them collaborate in a productive way?

GH: Usually we think there is one best architect for a particular site at a particular place. Sometimes we will narrow it down to a few and have a small competition and say, "Here is five thousand or ten thousand dollars apiece—draw us some sketches on an eight-and-a-half-by-eleven." I used to get Philip Johnson to do it for me. I'd say, "Send it to me over the fax. I don't want any drawings. Just send me freehand sketches."

NR: How did you meet Philip Johnson and begin working with him?

NR: How do you approach designing with sustainability in terms of your clients, especially corporate ones, who just don't care?

SB: I might be a little bit naïve; my approach starts with the human being. It starts with how they might feel and what they expect from the working-living-travel environment. And what should we give them. I think creating work space has a lot to do with dignity and giving people satisfaction where they spend a good part of their waking time. One client didn't want operable windows because he said that bugs would come in. I didn't understand this. I asked him why he drove an SUV and was wearing Eddie Bauer clothes and why he wanted to be an outdoors person when he was afraid of bugs? My approach is not a very theoretical one, but maybe if I would have built less in the relatively short time of my career I would have worked more on theory. But I have been in the lucky situation that many ideas I have had, have been realized. And I always have clients who are willing to go on this adventure with me.

NR: That is so rare. How do you convince your clients to go with your ideas and experiment with something that is such a long-term investment?

SB: I don't experiment with their investments. After all, we try to achieve a common goal: They will get the very best for their money. I always try to take them on a journey, which we live through together. What architects tend to forget is that for clients like CEO Henri Termeer, of Genzyme, or Manfred Bodin, of Norddeutsche Landesbank, a new building is a once-in-a-lifetime adventure. You are there to develop ideas together and translate these into architecture. Most clients acknowledge this, since they understand that I wouldn't try to tell them how to run their business. If you do it right, they happily join you on the journey. It is all a process—the planning, designing, and building. I do not believe in the hero architect who just draws up a sketch and hands it down the line to have it built. Architecture is hard work by many people, and it takes a lot of communication.

NR: So the client gives you a great deal of freedom in the end?

SB: Freedom is not always the basis for a good building. Mutual understanding and the possibility to develop within a given brief is a good basis. The Hysolar Building, which my father designed, was

GH: He had visited Houston a lot and liked the city, so I asked him to design a three-building complex called Post Oak Central. I had also started on Pennzoil Place and needed a second anchor tenant. Philip said, "Why not do two buildings?" And I said, "You can't put two buildings on one block in Houston." And he drew me a sketch of two smaller buildings in counterpoint. Two 36-story buildings cost less to build and can be built faster. And we did get that second tenant and were able to give Zapata its own front door. That is an example of how good architecture worked to improve cost and efficiency. And Ada Louise Huxtable said it "broke out of the Miesian box."

NR: How did you combine tall buildings and corporate centers with your interest in green urban design? Where did that focus begin?

GH: We are trying to lead the industry on green building development. We have been keeping energy costs low in our buildings for forty years. One Shell Plaza, in Houston, was a very low-energy building and the tallest lightweight concrete building ever built—the tube-within-a-tube building—but it took three years to build. I told its engineer, Fazlur Khan, "Faz, that was great, but it cost us a lot of interest. Now let's come up with a design that we can do in two years." So we did a composite on the Control Data Corporation Building, also in Houston, which was twenty stories tall, and then One Shell Square, in New Orleans. Fazlur was a fantastic structural engineer and a dear, dear person, a great human being, and a great fertile mind; it was a great experience to work with him.

NR: You also focused on new kinds urban spaces with projects such as the Galleria, in Houston. What are some models for you in terms of great active public spaces?

GH: The Galleria taught us that the ice skating rink in the middle created a situation where people promenade to watch and that people and ice-skaters like to be watched. For me, Europe is more of a place for pedestrians and public transportation. Cities like Copenhagen, where one-third of the people commute by bicycle, one-third by public transportation, and one-third by automobile, are gradually squeezing the automobile down. America was developed around the automobile, which is a shame because we won't ever be able to undo that. China is trying to follow us, and that is not the right pattern.

Behnisch, Behnisch & Partner, entrance of the Norddeutsche Landesbank, Dusseldorf, Germany, 2003. The ground floor of the bank is a primary component of the program's progressive energy concept. The bank is situated between the edge of the central business district on the north and a residential area to the south. The building provides a transition between the residential and commercial neighborhood that is echoed in a similar interior transition between a porous ground floor (with restaurants, shops, and galleries) and the office tower that rises from a landscaped courtyard. The courtyard is designed to passively generate a microclimate of fresh air that then feeds the tower's double façade and cools the office floors. The microclimate in combination with a soil-heat exchange system meets all the demand for cooling in the building and eliminates the need for conventional air-conditioning.

Hellmuth, Obata & Kassabaum for Gerald D. Hines Interests, The Galleria, Houston, Texas, 1970. The Galleria in Houston is a 3 million-square-foot mixed-use complex located on a 52-acre site in southwest Houston. Inspired by the Galleria Vittorio Emanuele in Milan, Italy, the complex features over 300 stores and restaurants, two Westin Hotels, three office towers totaling in excess of 1 million square feet, an Olympic-size ice-skating rink, and the University Club, a private social and athletic club. Anchor stores for the retail portion of the complex include Neiman Marcus, Lord & Taylor, Saks Fifth Avenue, and Macy's.

always published as a deconstructivist building, but it was way before the movement emerged. The client said, "Give me three containers and leave me alone. I don't have any requirements; I just need a box and a desk." Suddenly you work very formally. I think that is one of the reasons why some American architects have a formal approach: They work on shell and core because their client isn't involved. I have never done a true spec building. I mostly work on competitions. Our offices, my father's and mine, combined, have done almost 140 buildings with only four direct commissions.

NR: But aren't competition submissions more work than direct commissions?

SB: They are, but if you are good it pays for itself with the prize money. You don't have to join any country clubs or golf clubs; you don't have to take your clients out for dinner. For us, it is worth it—and it is also our research lab. For example, the Norddeutsche Landesbank we pursued in our office for years and did it in different ways in competitions until we had it developed far enough and then met the right client.

NR: What is it like working with developers as opposed to working on a static cultural project or a private company that owns the building that it inhabits?

SB: Genzyme was a developer who did a competition and our L.A. lofts were also a competition. I think there is no such thing as "the developer," "the architect," or "the dentist." There are always good and bad ones. Developers work commercially, but so do some of my colleagues. The difference between good and bad people in most professions is not their ability to master the subject but their willingness or, better, their ambitions to achieve something higher, to do more than just the necessary.

Most of our clients discovered that quality and support for architecture are good business. The public client with projects driven by unambitious public servants has become a big problem lately. Where people can only gain by taking no risks and making no decisions, no decisions are made. The general idea is that nobody ever has been fired for not making any decision.

NR: What is your relationship with the developers in Russia? Have you been able to influence program and scheme?

NR: What would you like to see in China, a country where you are building quite a lot now, such as Embassy House and Park Avenue, the five apartment towers in Beijing?

GH: I think developing the infrastructure is critical, but mass transit and highway development is so expensive and it is driving up the price of steel. We are looking at projects in Shenzhen where 75 percent is being built as special economic zones. They lay out the red carpet for us because they like the quality of our work, but we are one little voice. China can get it done—it is a command society. It is not like India, which is more like the United States—a messy democracy. But the Indian people have such abundant natural resources and a wonderful education system. India will take off despite all the bureaucracy. We are now looking at a 25,000-acre project in Mumbai where 17 million people live. They would like to create an economic zone that would have its own government, no red tape, and free trade. We might get involved in building a bridge-and-highway system that is about 30 kilometers long and would cost $800 million. It is like Wall Street in 1850 and the East Side Highway was what created Manhattan, but this is creating Manhattan in Mumbai. But I don't know whether we can do it because putting the infrastructure in place would be risky.

Mumbai was developed from islands, and the fill is approximately one-to-two meters and that created a peninsula. The peninsula runs straight up, and it is chockablock full of the worst to the best: Slums next to apartment buildings worth 1 to 2 million rupees. In the special economic zone we could create a city-state, and we would be the government of that city-state. We would have our own police force, and they would assign a judge from the supreme court to handle all cases within that. It would be tax-free for twenty years, so goods could come in and out without any import duties. We control all the buildings permits; we can issue a building permit in one day. Today it takes 26 agencies in Mumbai to get a permit, and it usually takes one to two years. We have an opportunity to build industrial centers with the biggest container port in India right next to us. We hope we can create a sustainable environment in building. The first phase of 1,000 acres shows you the type of distribution of what we would hope to do. We are looking at different ways of commuting and the ability to go wherever you need to go on your bicycle and bus. I don't know if you have ever seen the mass-transit system in Mumbai or Delhi, but they are hanging out the windows. I mean it; they are full! This could be a

SB: The projects in Russia are usually quite different from projects in the U.S. or Europe. You are paid to do a study. Then the client tries to obtain a permit. If they get the permit, they either pursue the project themselves or sell it. The most powerful person in the process is the mayor, who will in the end make the decision if and how a project will be realized.

We are pursuing two projects in Moscow. The transport terminal is a 256,000-square-foot project, with a city terminal and check-in areas for the airports, hotels, offices, shopping malls, rental cars, bus terminal, etc. It is part of the new Moscow City project. We have received the mayor's agreement and permit, but our clients in this case are underfinanced and not very quick in putting together the financing for this project.

The other project is an upscale residential and office complex at Tsvetnoy Boulevard. Here, we have undertaken a concept study and the permitting process. The project should proceed soon. The only misfortune in Moscow right now is that commercial American firms are underbidding and ignoring copyright agreements, trying to realize these projects for 50 percent of the fees that good architects would request.

The relationship with the clients is, on the basis of working together, quite good. They seem to accept that architecture is an asset and might require some effort and money.

NR: What do you think of a developer building part of a city versus the city government, as in Milan?

SB: Cities will always be cities—not necessarily urban in the architectural sense, but cities. Developers might be able to create whole quarters of cities, but in the end a city is owned by its inhabitants, at least in democratic political systems. And the people create their own organizations and make their own rules.

There have been many experiments, always closely connected with political utopias. Morus, Campanella, Locke, and Spinoza analyzed and worked with the ideal society. And interestingly, it was always closely connected to urban living. Developers don't live an isolated life, they don't exist beyond our societies. They are part of it and, depending on the economic system, provide an important substantial challenge to us. But in the industrial area, you even have a situation, if they allow you, you are like a utility.

NR: You are planning a development for a large-scale project in Libya, but where is the market for you there?

GH: Libya is extremely . . . let's just say it is going to be very difficult to build there. There are no indigenous workers at all, and we are trying to work out how we could bring them in. It will be one of the more difficult places, but I think it can be done; the market is huge. They are going to increase oil production from 1 million barrels a day to 5 million in the near future, but this is the first iteration, and we will see how it comes together. So there are some interesting situations that will challenge our firm for the next few years.

NR: When you walk around a city, do you look at potentials, ideas, or missed opportunities? Are there inspirations that you bring from one place to another?

GH: I look at how the cornice line is working or the quality of light. Or I think, if we built this in India, how would we do it? Or, I really like that rail line they have in Copenhagen; people can bring their bikes aboard—isn't that terrific? And in a poorer area, bikes are the sustainable way to commute. Wouldn't that be an exciting way to make a community, where you bike and then have a long spine on a low headway? You could start it with a bus, and then you could have a five-minute headway working it down to three minutes, and it could be used traveling the 22 to 30 kilometers to Mumbai. Wouldn't that be terrific? But you can't take bikes to Mumbai because there are no bike paths. But there would be one in ours. Those are the kinds of things I think about and also saw in Jan Gehl's Copenhagen projects. We are going to have him work on Garibaldi Repubblica to see how to generate the public spaces before we do the overall plan.

NR: What is your interest in teaching real estate development to architects?

GH: You always learn something from the students; they are great young minds to interact with. You learn something with every encounter—and that is what life is about. With the Urban Land Institute we service. Like phone companies, like service stations, like realtors and banks. They are part of the service infrastructure our societies have created or have allowed to develop. Thus, if development companies go too far, creating their own reality by sidestepping or misusing our political systems, their efforts must be curtailed. That's the job of our judicial systems. Maybe some developments went politically or morally wrong. I am of the opinion that "Celebration," the Disney Town, is tacky, absolutely inhumane, and fake. But so are some guarded residences in Bel Air.

NR: If this is really all about the bottom line and profit, how do you think developers can work on more up-to-date designs and still sell space rather than go for the standard sellable product?

SB: Developers are often financial people and thus rather conservative. The conservative and traditional approach to profit is short term and based on past experiences. A time span bears risks, and so people try to reduce any time span to the minimum. I am convinced that with the changes in our environment and our energy situation, political changes will come. Our societies will change as does our perception of qualities. Developers will feel the problem that qualities, sustained qualities, will become an issue. Some good clients have undertaken this already and act accordingly.

NR: In some of your work you have begun to look at prefabrication, such as the IBN Institute, in Wageningen, or the Linear City Lofts, in Los Angeles. Can you then create a prefab building system with sustainable building elements that can be integrated into the building industry?

SB: I believe that the development of the 1980s hybrid, prefab multipurpose building was never brought to a solution. This ridiculous movement of postmodernism, which I think is just a big accident of architectural history, cut it off. Postmodernism was a turn-of-the-century movement a few years too early, and they were wrongly motivated. What we did in the IBN Institute with mass-production elements, with "ready-mades," showed that these are efficient and have minimal energy and material use, so they do have something to do with sustainability. Architecturally, I am intrigued by the idea. What Kenzo Tange tried to achieve in the 1960s with his plug-in ideas has a big future, because sustainability is also about reusing buildings and the multiple use of buildings or their structures. One idea I have would be to create a parking garage that could be used as housing, a shopping mall,

sponsor annual design competitions with teams from different schools in an interdisciplinary setting. That is what happens in real life, except that the developer or the city takes the lead. The students then begin to understand the development process and how to improve the built environment. That is what we are all about and that is my purpose: to create great spaces and improve the quality of the built environment.

NR: How have you used the idea of icon and image in building a new project? For example, with the Garibaldi Repubblica project in Milan?

GH: I think that it is important for there to be something iconic about the project. To find something to distinguish the fashion center and the museum and the school—that in some way it could express that this was Milan. I can't describe it, but if I see it, I'll know it. Physically it could come in a lot of forms. It could come in the palette, in the shape of it, it could come in the color. It could come in a lot of different ways. That is one of the things we thought would be interesting about the studio at Yale, to test those ways. It will be interesting to see what happens when they put the project out to competition—what is it going to be? But of course, behind all of this is a selfish idea. The more identity that we can get from MOdAM, the more identity we could give to the development. Identity is something that is so essential to the value, momentum, and the perception of a project in the marketplace. This was, you could say, our ulterior motive here.

NR: During the studio there was much talk of the "value of design." In your project, what are some examples of the impact of good design?

GH: One great example for us, where we really have seen the value of design, is 53rd Street and Third Avenue in Manhattan, the Lipstick Building by Philip Johnson. In that area, you have a group of buildings that are rectangular, then all of a sudden here comes a building with a different shape that sets it apart. When we went to sell it, we were not forced to compete on the price because it had established itself so well in the New York market. They paid a very high cap rate for it—an extremely high price. So what you could call the "value of design" really, in that situation, came to be very important in the liquidating value of the property.

or office building, or an office building that could be reused as a shopping mall or as a parking garage, because in the end we will have too many parking garages. This would be about rethinking the idea of hybrids in a very practical way.

NR: Can you imagine taking whole areas and retooling them into sustainable developments?

SB: Maybe we should consider this on the basis of a vital city. New York is actually efficient and relatively sustainable because of its high density. The disastrous attack on Lower Manhattan would have been a chance to rethink the separation of working and living. We live in a postindustrial or knowledge-based society. Our way of living and our economies are changing more rapidly than economists will acknowledge. Our stock exchange system is outdated because it is industrially based. We have tried to use it for the yahoos of the new market and it failed enormously. More stock values were destroyed than in any economic crash in history. And we keep ignoring the changes. Considering that master planning takes ten to twenty years and that a building is developed over three to five years, we are speculating about developments that we can't know or understand—we are like fortune-tellers. So change, reuse, and flexible infrastructure become significant. The example of Lower Manhattan shows that there is a chance, even though caused by a disastrous act of violence, to make a part of the city fit for the future and not just a rebuilding of the past.

NR: What do you think of the idea of icon buildings or signature buildings that then become a draw for a developer's project?

SB: Icon buildings can support a new development, create whole new quarters, regenerate whole regions. Often a landmark is content-driven, not architecture-driven, such as the Monterey Aquarium. Though in my opinion it is a fine piece of architecture, its strength and meaning are based on being a fantastic aquarium at a great location in a good set of buildings rather than being a single landmark building. Bilbao is different, but not to be repeated.

The wish to create a landmark as the initial building for a great, successful new development is understandable, but not necessarily successful. If a client has the attitude that the effort undertaken to

NR: How do you think developers can work better with architects? What kind of example do you hope to set in your new work?

GH: I certainly think there can be new types of collaboration. We consider the architects to be our partners in the concept and the programming. A good example was when Gyo Obata [HOK], our architect for the Galleria, in Houston, suggested that to animate the big basement space we put in an ice-skating rink. And I said, "An ice-skating rink, in Houston, Texas?" That was really extraordinary. What is important is to have the sense that you are going to try to do something interesting. That is what we have enjoyed. It's adding another major member to the team.

NR: What is the importance of sustainability in your projects today?

GH: For a lot of our new projects we are trying to go for, say, a LEED ranking of bronze to gold in most situations. In London, for example, you can do a lot more because the cost of the buildings are so high. You can only do as much as possible within the boundaries of the financial envelope. We are very interested in sustainability from the point of view of achieving a lower operating cost and a lower renovation cost.

What we saw in India recently was that they build pretty inexpensively, and they get them up in six months. What they are doing there is to only raise the floors for the server rooms, but the rest are not raised at all. They run everything over the ceiling, then drop into the columns and then spread out to the workstations. It gives a little more height to the space. What we did at Shell was to build some extra façade, but the additional cost of the façade was very small in comparison with the savings in the mechanical systems and the increased flexibility that it gave us. There are no sacred cows. The more space you have in a building the better—where you can distribute horizontally on a floor or vertically—it gives you a lot more flexibility for changes and for keeping a building modern. But you also may lose some net rentable area. You have to watch out and figure out the right balance.

NR: Why are you in the business of development and what are you ultimate goals?

create a good or even outstanding building is enough for a whole development, he is bound to fail. The Guggenheim in Bilbao was in a given urban setting. A new development will always be the backdrop against which such a token landmark building will be judged.

NR: What about the stylistic deconstructivist issue in your work and that of your father? How did that help or hinder you? Did it have any meaning for you or did the critics brand you as such?

SB: This was at a time when I just started working in my father's office. He was branded as deconstructivist. I was generally sensitive on this issue until I read about Derrida's ideas. I then noticed that deconstructivism in architecture came ten years late–it is not just about odd angles. I feel more comfortable with chaos theory as a basic explanation for life. Some of my father's buildings from the 1960s and 1970s are seemingly decon in look. But I don't think we fit that description, in terms of meaning. Our approach is to find the appropriate or best possible solution considering many aspects of architecture and then look at the humanistic and functional side.

NR: Is that organic design in the holistic sense of architecture developing naturally from its circumstances and context, rather from preconceived ideas about style and design?

SB: That is a nice question. I like that idea. But it is not organic as we normally see it architecturally, but rather as a philosophical question or motivation. It could be organic if you think how organic things develop. I like "expressionistic" as a term more than "deconstructivist." Our basis would be Scharoun. The architecture, the space, and appearance of buildings express forces that are not always obvious and have to be interpreted, understood. The influences that work in this environment, climate, and function are able to express themselves in the building. So other forces help form the building and maybe express themselves in a rather surprising way. It is a different, indirect, not so obvious kind of functionalism. Maybe that is it.

GH: It is fun to be in a business that you are passionate about, and I think if you are not passionate, get out of that business. I think developers have a chance to improve the built environment; you do have to work in the context of an economic sense of whatever the project is. Yes, it's tougher because you can't just draw something and accept it as a client. A good client is a client who challenges the architect, who creates the challenge. This is where you can make something better together. I think those are the things that are important. If we can build better cities and a better environment, then we will leave this planet better than we found it.

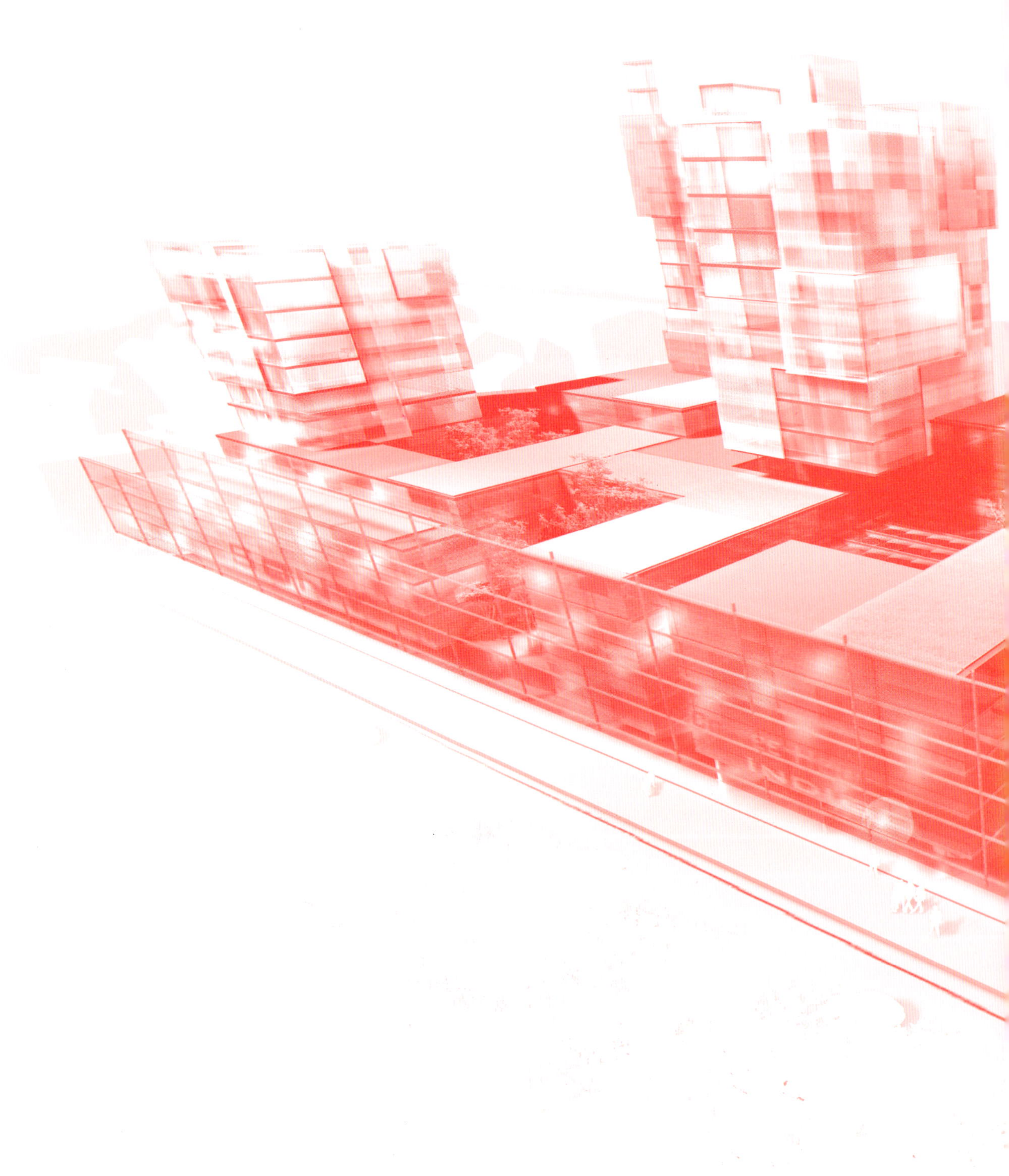

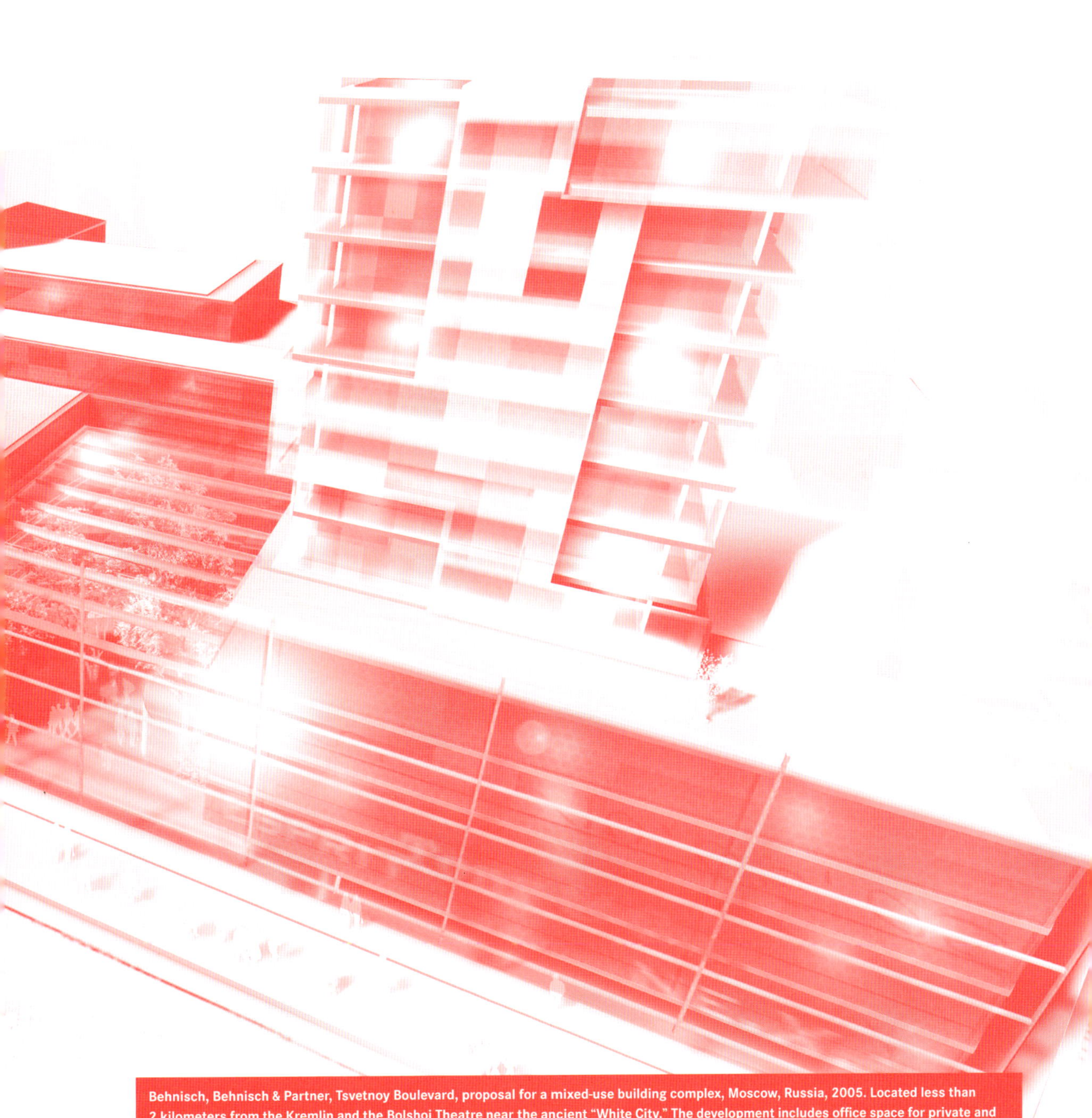

Behnisch, Behnisch & Partner, Tsvetnoy Boulevard, proposal for a mixed-use building complex, Moscow, Russia, 2005. Located less than 2 kilometers from the Kremlin and the Bolshoi Theatre near the ancient "White City." The development includes office space for private and governmental use, luxury residential space, ground-floor retail space, and a metro terminal.

Hines Completed Projects

53rd At Third Avenue, John Burgee Architects with Philip Johnson, New York, NY

Del Bosque, Cesar Pelli & Associates, Mexico City, Mexico

DZ Bank, Frank O. Gehry & Associates, Berlin, Germany

Sugar Land, TX
A 9,700-acre
master-planned community

Diagonal Mar Center, Robert A. M. Stern Architects, Barcelona, Spain

Tour EDF, Pei, Cobb Freed & Partners, Paris, France

Metropolitan, Foster and Partners, Warsaw, Poland

Diagonal Mar Residential, architects include Oscar Tusquets,
Jacobs Sereland, EDAW, Kaufman & Meeks, Muñoz + Albin, Barcelona, Spain

1990s

2000–present

Office
Residential
Retail
Mixed Use
Other (Inc. Industrial, Institutional)

The A+D Studio at Yale: Markus Dochantschi Garibaldi Repubblica, a current development project by Hines in Milan, was the site where Yale students were asked to design a project that focused on a 100,000-square-foot Fashion Museum and School for the Foundation of Fashion, Design, and Communication (Fondazione della moda, design e comunicazione, or MOdAM) that will be presented as a major international design competition within the next year. Students were asked to conceptualize and design the MOdAM. Throughout the design process, they worked closely with the Hines organization—the client—to learn about a developer's goals and needs, seeking to elaborate ideas for the criteria of function, program, construction techniques, and profit; the latter not being typically considered in design studios of architecture schools. The studio dynamic aimed to create a new working dialogue between designers and developers, transforming expectations and finding strategies for collaboration that would simultaneously produce exceptional architecture and a profitable commercial development.

As the students worked to understand the confluence of programmatic and financial concerns, the developer embraced and challenged unconventional (contemporary) design ideas while developing a new understanding of the value of design; a way to give scientific precision to what is commonly referred to as the "Bilbao effect." How do we measure the value of successful, innovative architecture? Is it as a marketing tool, an icon, the return on capital investment, the satisfaction of the tenants, or perhaps its ecological sustainability? Buildings as diverse as Norman Foster's Swiss Re, in London; Stefan Behnisch's Genzyme Building, in Cambridge; Zaha Hadid's Rosenthal Contemporary Art Center, in Cincinnati; and Gerald Hines' residential development with Jean Nouvel, in New York, provided models for the student work.

Lately, the modern developer and corporation have begun to place value (financial and social) on unusual architectural design. Corporations have started to acknowledge that there is a connection between architecture and their employees' well-being. Productivity has been shown to dramatically increase in high-quality buildings that are comfortable and filled with light and air. While this is not a new phenomenon, in the past decade corporations such as Hearst, Vitra, Mercedes, BMW, and institutions from museums to schools, which own their properties rather than just lease office space, see a long-term investment in architecture as both a marketing tool and a symbol of permanence.

As the boundaries between architecture, economics, and marketing blur, the profession has exacted a more intensive collaboration between architect and developer. While direct costs per square foot and anticipated re-sale value can be closely monitored and even projected, the added value of design quality remains unquantifiable and hypothetical. The role of the architect as solely a designer is shrinking, demanding architects to become generalists and partners in development, incorporating economics into their buildings, and using design as a powerful economic multiplier. Developer buildings are beginning to shift away from a separation between design excellence and economic success and are more often seen as a three-dimensional marketing tool.

But can architects capitalize on profits by dramatically increasing revenues through design? How would we quantify this? How does one know that value is being added (as defined by an architect or developer) in the right places? Architects can maximize store frontages, direct pedestrian flow, and strategically design space that a developer's market analysis has revealed will maximize profits. But will this conflict with a larger design agenda envisioned by the architect? Thus, in the end, how can the architectural profession make practical this expansive awareness? As the insight into point of view and developer's demands heighten the awareness of the designer, the design concept becomes inseparable from the business concept. In the Yale studio, students saw how opportunities for increased collaboration are essential in today's economic and environmentally fragile environment and learned furthermore how to implement such knowledge to enhance both design quality and economic profitability.

Studio Brief

MOdAM will consist of two distinct programs: a fashion museum and a fashion school, joined in a single building. The fashion museum will be an extension of the Foundation of Fashion in Milan. It will not have a permanent archive but will host temporary exhibitions on all aspects of fashion and fashion culture, with a particular emphasis on collaborations between fashion and the fine arts, music, cinema, dance, and theater. MOdAM will be more an incubator than a museum, intended to simulate the culture of fashion in Milan.

The fashion school, Scuola di Alta Formazione (or MOdAM-Formazione), will be a collaboration between three universities in Milan: Università Bocconi, for economics and business management; Politechnico, for design; and Università Cattolica, for the social sciences. At MOdAM, the three universities will offer a unique interdisciplinary fashion management degree, the first of its kind in Italy. The new university will focus on new business models and organizational strategies for the fashion industry, incorporating the full production cycle from design to manufacturing, marketing, and retail.

The studio began with a trip to the site in Milan, along with meetings with Hines and key personnel in his local office as well as officials from city government, museum directors, and representatives of the fashion industry, including Beatrice Trussardi (CEO of Trussardi group and vice president of the Foundation of Fashion), Franka Sozzani (editor in chief, *Vogue Italia*), and Gianna Verga, city planner for Milan. The students were asked to consider not only the immediate infrastructure and surrounding urban fabric but also to analyze and quantify "Italian lifestyle." Back in the studio, students analyzed the proposed program and Cesar Pelli's Master Plan.

The students were able to challenge the brief based on a sensitive synthesis between the needs of the school/museum and the potential for the school/museum, always with an eye toward an income-generating program (e.g., to what extent could a museum store in a fashion museum become a boutique—without selling out?). In noting that fashion and architecture share common ground, the students were asked to research and juxtapose fabric/material, trend/style, haute couture/custom, mass production/prefabrication, brand designer/signature architect, smart clothing/smart building. Basic parameters were established: The museum and school must work together. The museum will not only exhibit current fashion, fashion collections from established designers, and history, but also create a forum for the fashion students' work. In the development of the design, the students discussed how such a connection could work and what synergies could be created.

Throughout the semester, the students had reviews with their professors—Stefan Behnisch, Gerald Hines, Jay Wyper, managing director of Hines Europe, and Markus Dochantschi of studioMDA—as well as environmental consultants, such as Thomas Auer of TransSolar. Gerald Hines acted as the building owner for the studio, explaining to the students his expectations. Students were asked to reconcile a complex set of ambitions: for Hines, an icon that would give a strong identity for Garibaldi Repubblica; for the Foundation of Fashion, an unprecedented center for fashion and contemporary culture in Milan; and for the city of Milan, a public amenity that would reconnect the Garibaldi Repubblica to the surrounding neighborhood's civic life.

The studio projects answered questions and pursued ideas about ways to locate the museum, provide public programming, and integrate the cultural and educational program of MOdAM with the new commercial development that will surround it. Some students decided to substantially revise the Pelli Master Plan, while others focused on more incremental adjustments. Two sides of the urban development were explored: on one hand, the perspective of the developer and urban economists concerned with a profitable commercial development and, on the other, the creation of a new major public space for fashion and culture in Milan. Fashion and finance marked the two extremes of a spectrum for research in the studio. Using sources as diverse as garment construction, fashion marketing strategies, revenue pro formas, and infrastructure design, the studio sought ways to identify an architectural typology for the fashion museum and school that would bring together contemporary culture and commerce. Form was often inspired by fashion, including its use of image, decorative surfaces, and weaving and textile design, which in several projects led to innovative ideas about building enclosure as a performative skin that could adapt to the underlying building in a way similar to how a garment adapts to a human body. Program was more often under the influence of finance, as studies of circulation, demographics, and revenue profiles led to experiments in the programmatic organization of MOdAM.

As seen in the following pages, students addressed the question of value in architecture in many ways. They addressed issues of the site and urban planning in teams by analyzing the master plan's organization; then they prepared studies for the development of the open space, the circulation, and infrastructure; and finally, they worked closely on the development of the specific building design, exploring techniques of enclosure, surface performance, lifestyle, and iconic form. Some presented architecture as a fully quantifiable economic metric; others suggested that the real strength of architecture is found in its more elusive qualities, such as atmosphere, effect, and a unique sense of space. With developers taking on the role of professors, students were also required to have rigorous answers to pragmatic concerns, such as leasable floor area, expected demographics, pedestrian circulation, access, security, links to existing infrastructure, requirements for new capital investment in infrastructure, project life-cycle costs, operating expenses, the capacity for flexible programming, and, of course, parking.

The design of a center for fashion and culture in Milan provided a forum for in-depth research into an architecture that combines formal and programmatic experimentation with the exacting measures of profit and function. The students used the logic of a developer to find new aesthetic solutions and, inversely, the economic potential of formal intuition. Above all, the client asked for something remarkable, a new icon for fashion in Milan stitched into the existing fabric of the city.

MOdAM Museum	Occupancy	Area (in square feet)
4 galleries (7,500 square feet each)		30,000
Cinema	150	3,200
Technical laboratory		500
Digital video and film room		1,500
Internet area		500
Learning center		1,000
Library		3,200
Bookstore		2,150
TOTAL		42,050 square feet

MOdAM Formazione	Occupancy	Area (in square feet)
Lecture halls		
6 General purpose classrooms	50	5,000
2 Design rooms	50	5,000
8 Practice rooms	25	4,000
4 Lecture rooms for small groups	75	4,800
3 Design laboratories		4,500
2 Double-height laboratory		
(retail, editing/publishing/photography)		6,000
2 Computer centers		
(languages, information technology)	50	2,000
Library	100	5,000
Great Hall		7,000
Offices and mobile work stations		4,000
TOTAL		47,300 square feet

Yale Student Design Strategies Yale students devised master-plan strategies to establish sensitive programming of the site from the perspective of the developer, resulting in two systems, EasyPlan and Pixelation.

EasyPlan A prototype software program that combines the perspective of a real estate developer with the master-plan design process of an architect. The software is designed to evaluate the financial implications of an architectural strategy and the spatial implications of a project's economic strategy. EasyPlan offers a means to quantify the impact of architecture on a project's bottom line and refine that impact to maximize the positive value of the design. As a tool for architects, the economic analysis provided by EasyPlan certainly cannot be a substitute for more conventional metrics of architectural quality. However, the goal of EasyPlan is to show that many of these qualities, especially urban products like an active and healthy public realm, are often also the best way to maximize the profitability of a development.

To input information into the program, the user clicks on regions of a site plan to assign uses (office, residential, etc.) to that area, then enters the total quantity of each use for the entire project, which is distributed evenly over the designated regions on the site plan. Next, the software runs a simulation of a typical 24-hour period, tracking a theoretical demographic make-up and circulation flows of the project based on the spatial organization in the master plan. The result is then used to assemble a two-part revenue profile. The first part is the total direct revenue of the project; the second is the total indirect revenue, which is a measure of all rent premiums that the project achieves. Indirect revenue is a surcharge on revenue paid by one component of a project to be near another. In essence, it is the value of location. Different uses have a different capability to generate indirect revenue, just as different users are more willing to pay a premium than others. For instance, at Garibaldi Repubblica, the fashion museum generates indirect revenue because it has the capacity to draw a particular demographic in high numbers, and the retail stores are willing to pay a premium to be near that demographic. EasyPlan allows the architect to identify scenarios that maximize the indirect revenue-gain profile and thereby more fully coordinate the components of the project into a dynamic whole. Indirect revenue is a measure of the degree to which a collection of buildings is able to add up to more than the sum of its parts. It is a measure of positive interaction, of an emerging community, a vital urban space.

MOdAM Museum Space

	PROGRAM SIZE # Rooms	SM/Room	Total SM	PEOPLE People/Room*	People/SM	Total People	% Total	WEEKDAY DEMOGRAPHICS (@ optimal occupancy) % In-Transit	In-Transit	% Habitual	Habitual	% Non-Habitual	1.0 Non-Habitual	WEEKEND DEMOGRAPHICS (@90% optimal occupancy) % In-Transit	In-Transit	% Habitual	Habitual	% Non-Habitual	0.9 Non-Habitual
Galleries	4	700	2,800	150	0.21	600	57%	0.0%	0	10.0%	60	90.0%	540	0.0%	0	2.0%	10	90.0%	437
Cinema	1	300	300	150	0.50	150	14%	0.0%	0	10.0%	15	90.0%	135	0.0%	0	2.0%	2	90.0%	109
Technical Laboratory	1	100	100	20	0.20	20	2%	0.0%	0	2.0%	0	98.0%	20	0.0%	0	2.0%	0	98.0%	17
Digital Video and Film Room	1	300	300	150	0.50	150	14%	0.0%	0	2.0%	3	98.0%	147	0.0%	0	2.0%	3	98.0%	130
Internet Area	1	100	100	60	0.60	60	6%	2.0%	1	10.0%	6	88.0%	53	2.0%	1	2.0%	1	88.0%	42
Learning Center	1	100	100	20	0.20	20	2%	0.0%	0	2.0%	0	98.0%	20	0.0%	0	2.0%	0	98.0%	17
Library	1	300	300	40	0.13	40	4%	0.0%	0	10.0%	4	90.0%	36	0.0%	0	2.0%	1	90.0%	29
Bookstore	1	200	200	15	0.08	15	1%	2.0%	0	10.0%	2	88.0%	13	2.0%	0	2.0%	0	88.0%	10
Total	**11**	**2,100**	**4,200**	**605**	**2.42**	**1,055**		**0.1%**	**2**	**8.6%**	**90**	**91.3%**	**963**	**0.5%**	**1**	**2.0%**	**17**	**92.5%**	**792**

MOdAM Training

	PROGRAM SIZE # Rooms	SM/Room	Total SM	PEOPLE People/Room*	People/SM	Total People	% Total	WEEKDAY DEMOGRAPHICS (@ optimal occupancy) % In-Transit	In-Transit	% Habitual	Habitual	% Non-Habitual	1.0 Non-Habitual	WEEKEND DEMOGRAPHICS (@20% optimal occupancy) % In-Transit	In-Transit	% Habitual	Habitual	% Non-Habitual	0.2 Non-Habitual
Classrooms	6	83	500	50	0.60	300	23%	0.0%	0	100.0%	300	0.0%	0	0.0%	0	100.0%	0	0.0%	0
Design Rooms	2	250	500	50	0.20	100	8%	0.0%	0	100.0%	100	0.0%	0	0.0%	0	100.0%	0	0.0%	0
Practice Rooms	8	50	400	25	0.50	200	15%	0.0%	0	100.0%	200	0.0%	0	0.0%	0	100.0%	0	0.0%	0
Lecture Rooms	4	88	350	60	0.69	240	18%	0.0%	0	80.0%	192	20.0%	48	0.0%	0	80.0%	8	20.0%	2
Labs	3	150	450	50	0.33	150	11%	0.0%	0	100.0%	150	0.0%	0	0.0%	0	100.0%	0	0.0%	0
Double Height Labs	2	300	600	50	0.17	100	8%	0.0%	0	100.0%	100	0.0%	0	0.0%	0	100.0%	0	0.0%	0
Computer Labs	2	100	200	50	0.50	100	8%	0.0%	0	100.0%	100	0.0%	0	0.0%	0	100.0%	0	0.0%	0
Library	1	300	300	100	0.33	100	8%	2.0%	2	80.0%	80	18.0%	18	2.0%	0	80.0%	3	18.0%	1
Great Hall	1	700	700	0	0.00	0	0%	0.0%	0	80.0%	0	20.0%	0	0.0%	0	80.0%	0	20.0%	0
Offices/Workstations	1	400	400	40	0.10	40	3%	0.0%	0	100.0%	40	0.0%	0	0.0%	0	100.0%	0	0.0%	0
Common Area	1	1,000	1,000	0	0.00	0	0%	2.0%	0	80.0%	0	18.0%	0	2.0%	0	80.0%	0	18.0%	0
Total	**31**	**3,421**	**5,400**	**475**	**3.42**	**1,330**		**0.2%**	**2**	**94.9%**	**1,262**	**5.0%**	**66**	**0.4%**	**0**	**92.7%**	**11**	**6.9%**	**3**

	PROGRAM SIZE # Rooms	SM/Room	Total SM	PEOPLE People/Room*	People/SM	Total People	% Total	WEEKDAY DEMOGRAPHICS (@ optimal occupancy) % In-Transit	In-Transit	% Habitual	Habitual	% Non-Habitual	1.0 Non-Habitual	WEEKEND DEMOGRAPHICS (@100% optimal occupancy) % In-Transit	In-Transit	% Habitual	Habitual	% Non-Habitual	1.0 Non-Habitual
MOdAM Exposition	**29**	**3,400**	**10,000**	**710**	**0.83**	**2,350**		**5.0%**	**118**	**5.0%**	**118**	**90.0%**	**2,115**	**5.0%**	**118**	**5.0%**	**118**	**90.0%**	**2,115**
Commercial	**54**	**4,620**	**50,060**	**180**	**0.20**	**1,896**		**0.0%**	**0**	**95.0%**	**1,801**	**5.0%**	**95**	**0.0%**	**0**	**98.0%**	**186**	**2.0%**	**4**
Residential	**18**	**560**	**10,080**	**28**	**0.05**	**504**		**0.0%**	**0**	**98.0%**	**494**	**2.0%**	**10**	**0.0%**	**0**	**98.0%**	**445**	**2.0%**	**9**
Hotel	**12**	**625**	**7,500**	**38**	**0.06**	**450**		**0.0%**	**0**	**4.0%**	**18**	**96.0%**	**432**	**0.0%**	**0**	**4.0%**	**18**	**96.0%**	**432**
Retail			**8,510**	**20**	**0.11**	**460**		**10.0%**	**46**	**20.0%**	**92**	**70.0%**	**322**	**10.0%**	**46**	**20.0%**	**92**	**70.0%**	**322**
Parking	**2,000**	**39**	**77,400**	**1.5**	**0.04**	**3,000**		**0.0%**	**0**	**80.0%**	**2,400**	**20.0%**	**600**	**0.0%**	**0**	**10.0%**	**180**	**90.0%**	**1620**
Plinth Total			**38,676**																
Program Total			**173,150**			**11,045**		**1.5%**	**167**	**56.8%**	**6,275**	**41.7%**	**4,603**	**1.5%**	**165**	**9.6%**	**1,066**	**48.0%**	**5,297**

MOdAM Museum Space

	OPTIMAL OPERATING HOURS Start Operating Hours	End Operating Hours	Total Hours	OPTIMAL REVENUE GENERATED Direct Revenue/SM	Direct Revenue/Hour	Direct Revenue	Indirect Revenue/SM	Indirect Revenue/Hour	Indirect Revenue	Revenue Bonus	Total Revenue
Galleries	9:00	18:00	9:00	€0.00	€0.00	€0.00	€1.99	€620.16	€5,581.48	100%	€5,581.48
Cinema	9:00	22:00	13:00	€0.00	€0.00	€0.00	€4.65	€107.34	€1,395.37	100%	€1,395.37
Technical Laboratory	9:00	17:00	8:00	€0.00	€0.00	€0.00	€1.86	€23.26	€186.05	100%	€186.05
Digital Video and Film Room	9:00	18:00	9:00	€0.00	€0.00	€0.00	€4.65	€155.04	€1,395.37	100%	€1,395.37
Internet Area	9:00	17:00	8:00	€0.00	€0.00	€0.00	€5.58	€69.77	€558.15	100%	€558.15
Learning Center	9:00	17:00	8:00	€0.00	€0.00	€0.00	€1.86	€23.26	€186.05	100%	€186.05
Library	9:00	17:00	8:00	€0.00	€0.00	€0.00	€1.24	€46.51	€372.10	100%	€372.10
Bookstore	9:00	18:00	9:00	€600.00	€10,322.58	€120,000.00	€0.70	€15.50	€139.54	0%	€120,139.54
Total	**9:00**	**18:00**	**9:00**			**€120,000.00**	**€2.34**	**€844.22**	**€9,814.10**	**8%**	**€129,814.10**

MOdAM Training

	OPTIMAL OPERATING HOURS Start Operating Hours	End Operating Hours	Total Hours	OPTIMAL REVENUE GENERATED Direct Revenue/SM	Direct Revenue/Hour	Direct Revenue	Indirect Revenue/SM	Indirect Revenue/Hour	Indirect Revenue	Revenue Bonus	Total Revenue
Classrooms	9:00	18:00	9:00	€0.00	€0.00	€0.00	€0.03	€1.60	€14.37	100%	€14.37
Design Rooms	10:00	23:00	13:00	€0.00	€0.00	€0.00	€0.01	€0.37	€4.79	100%	€4.79
Practice Rooms	10:00	23:00	13:00	€0.00	€0.00	€0.00	€0.02	€0.74	€9.58	100%	€9.58
Lecture Rooms	9:00	18:00	9:00	€0.00	€0.00	€0.00	€0.03	€1.28	€11.50	100%	€11.50
Labs	9:00	18:00	9:00	€0.00	€0.00	€0.00	€0.02	€0.80	€7.19	100%	€7.19
Double Height Labs	9:00	18:00	9:00	€0.00	€0.00	€0.00	€0.01	€0.53	€4.79	100%	€4.79
Computer Labs	9:00	23:00	14:00	€0.00	€0.00	€0.00	€0.02	€0.34	€4.79	100%	€4.79
Library	9:00	17:00	8:00	€0.00	€0.00	€0.00	€0.02	€0.60	€4.79	100%	€4.79
Great Hall	9:00	23:00	14:00	€0.00	€0.00	€0.00	€0.00	€0.00	€0.00	0%	€0.00
Offices/Workstations	9:00	17:00	8:00	€0.00	€0.00	€0.00	€0.00	€0.24	€1.92	100%	€1.92
Common Area	9:00	23:00	14:00	€0.00	€0.00	€0.00	€0.00	€0.00	€0.00	0%	€0.00
Total	**9:10**	**20:05**	**10:54**			**€0.00**	**€0.01**	**€4.52**	**€63.72**	**100%**	**€63.72**

	OPTIMAL OPERATING HOURS Start Operating Hours	End Operating Hours	Total Hours	OPTIMAL REVENUE GENERATED Direct Revenue/SM	Direct Revenue/Hour	Direct Revenue	Indirect Revenue/SM	Indirect Revenue/Hour	Indirect Revenue	Revenue Bonus	Total Revenue
MOdAM Exposition	**9:00**	**21:00**	**12:00**			**€3,720,000.00**	**€2.04**	**€1,317.90**	**€20,427.38**	**1%**	**€3,740,427.38**
Commercial	**9:00**	**18:00**	**9:00**			**€831,600.00**	**€0.05**	**€234.81**	**€2,729.66**	**0%**	**€834,329.66**
Residential	**7:00**	**23:00**	**16:00**			**€1,680,000.00**	**€0.04**	**€21.07**	**€435.46**	**0%**	**€1,680,435.46**
Hotel	**6:00**	**23:00**	**17:00**			**€3,750,000.00**	**€0.61**	**€208.29**	**€4,573.80**	**0%**	**€3,754,573.80**
Retail	**9:00**	**18:00**	**9:00**			**€222,000.00**	**€0.17**	**€121.68**	**€1,414.50**	**1%**	**€223,414.50**
Parking	**8:00**	**23:00**	**15:00**			**€92,880.00**	**€0.09**	**€362.32**	**€7,020.00**	**7%**	**€99,900.00**
Plinth Total											
Program Total						**€10,416,480.00**			**€46,478.62**		**€10,462,958.62**

$$\text{Direct Revenue} = \text{Market Rent} + \text{Indirect Revenue}$$

$$\text{Indirect Revenue} = \sum (S_i + E_i \ldots + P_i)$$

EXAMPLE:

$$M_{indirect} = S^{i}_{m} + E^{i}_{m} + C^{i}_{m} + Res^{i}_{m} + H^{i}_{m} + Ret^{i}_{m} + P^{i}_{m}$$

where

$$S_m = \text{indirect revenue to school from museum} = ((.2P_{in\ transit} + 1P_{habitual} + 5P_{nonhabitual}) * z^s)$$

DIRECT / INDIRECT REVENUE DEFINITION

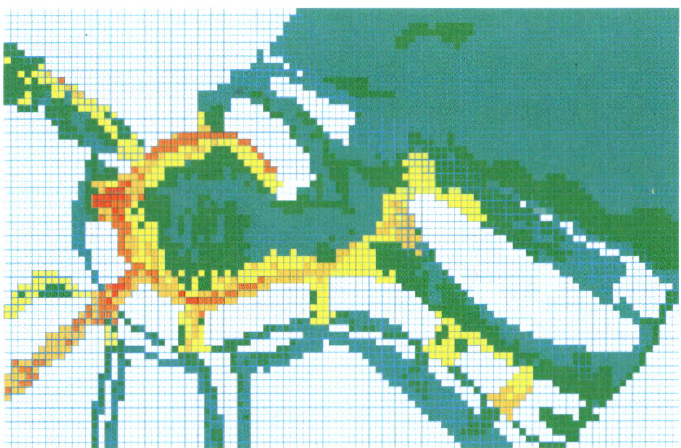

CIRCULATION STUDY PELLI CLARKE PELLI MASTER PLAN

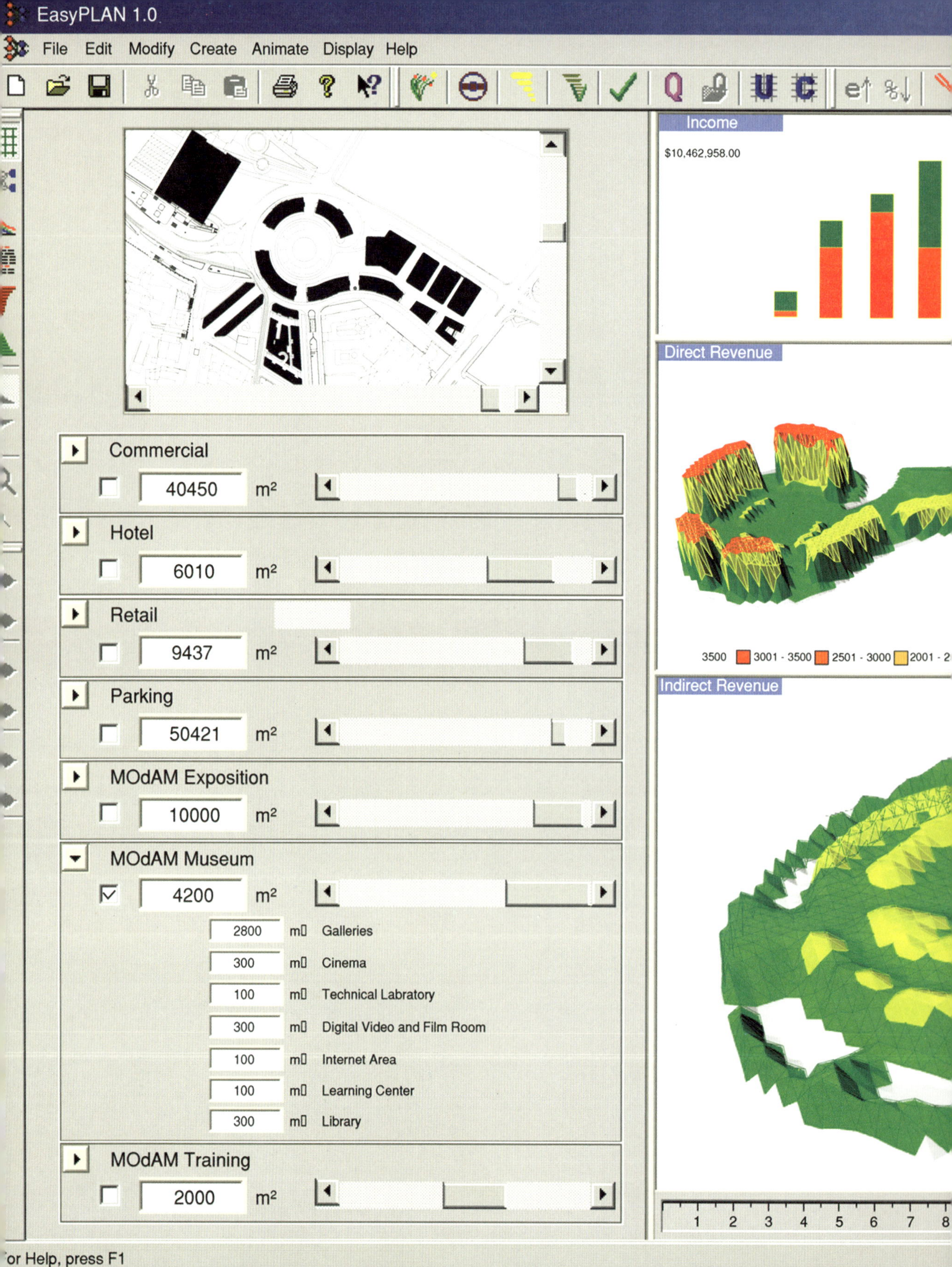

EasyPLAN 1.0
File
Edit
Modify
Create
Animate
Display
Help
Income
$10,462,958.00
Direct Revenue
3500
3001 - 3500
2501 - 3000
2001 - 2
Indirect Revenue
1
2
3
4
5
6
7
8
Commercial
40450
m²
Hotel
6010
m²
Retail
9437
m²
Parking
50421
m²
MOdAM Exposition
10000
m²
MOdAM Museum
4200
m²
2800 m Galleries
300 m Cinema
100 m Technical Labratory
300 m Digital Video and Film Room
100 m Internet Area
100 m Learning Center
300 m Library
MOdAM Training
2000
m²
or Help, press F1

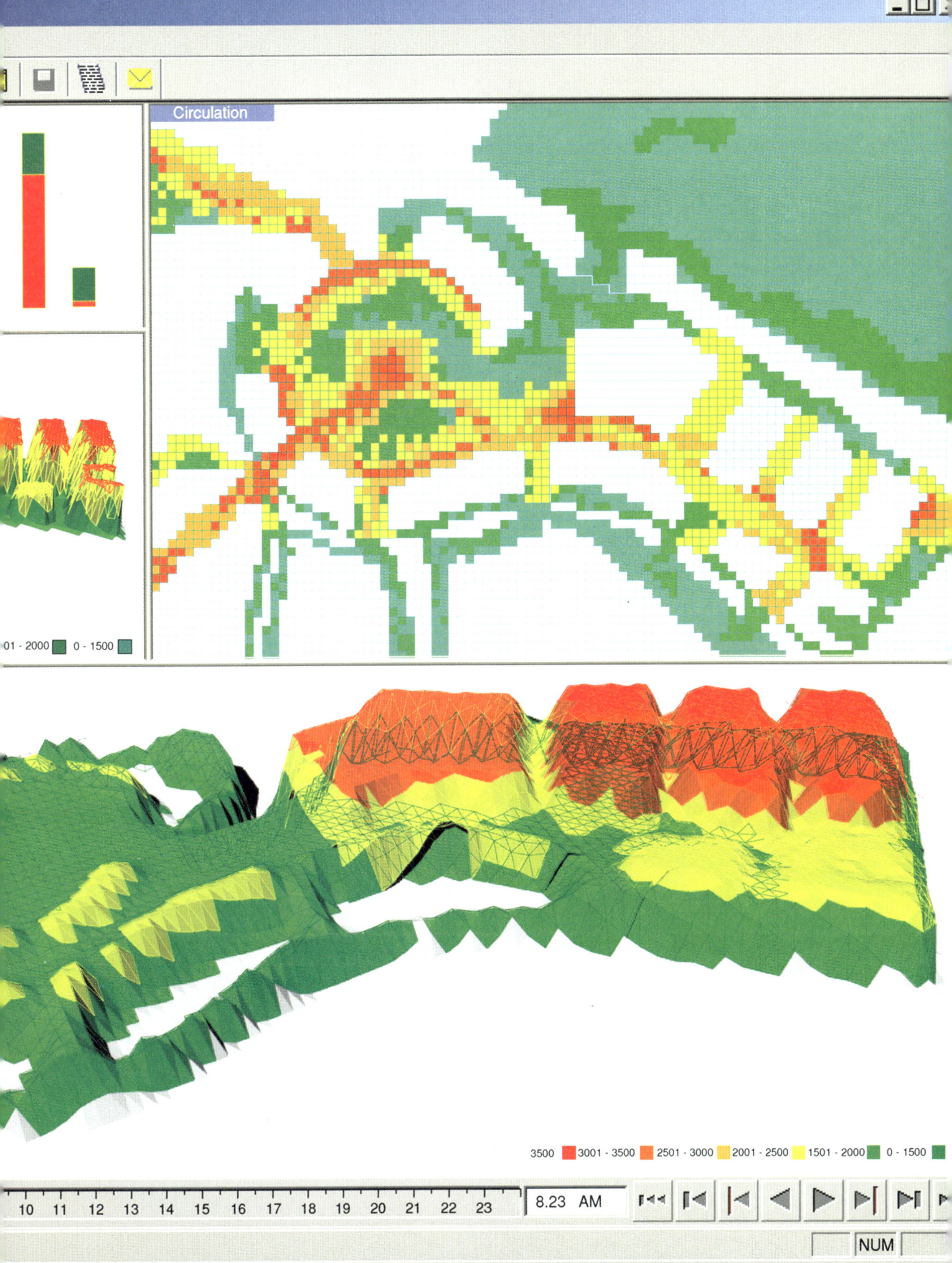

Circulation
01 - 2000
0 - 1500
3500
3001 - 3500
2501 - 3000
2001 - 2500
1501 - 2000
0 - 1500
10
11
12
13
14
15
16
17
18
19
20
21
22
23
8.23 AM
NUM

Pixelation The pixel as a design strategy. A pixel, short for "picture element," is a single point of color in a digital image. It is the smallest indivisible component of the image, like an atom of matter in a philosophical sense: pure matter not composed of anything else. The pixel-image relationship is a matter of assembly. Every digital image is nothing more than a collection of pixels. A higher-resolution image simply has more pixels than a lower-resolution version of the same image. There is no intermediary organization. One either has the smallest part or the largest whole.

The pixel initially was the basis of a programming experiment. A set of activities was extracted from the functional requirements for MOdAM. Each activity was considered a single pixel with a hexagonal shape, so that a single "activity-pixel" could be combined with up to six other activities. Combinations of pixels produced new program typologies as mixing colored paint produces tints and hues: For example, five pixels, each 25 square meters of library space, could be mixed with three pixels of café program and six pixels of design studio. Sets of these new typologies were then grouped together to form a program layout for MOdAM. Because these arrangements were purely organizational, it was easy to extend the program groups of the building into the full surface area of the Garibaldi Repubblica site; the programming of MOdAM seamlessly merged into urban design. With the site now a continuous pixel program grid, the difference between building and landscape was practically meaningless. The lines of a plan could be drawn any number of ways, cutting buildings, pavilions, and open space out of the same program fabric. As buildings emerged from this soup of program, the make-up of their component typologies were used to define architectonic qualities, including the structural grid, the placement of apertures, and the degree of permeability to neighboring program types—from the organization came the architecture.

Garibaldi

	sq.m.
Park	100,000
Commercial	50,000
Parking (inc. Museum & School)	46,200
Expo Center	20,000
admissions	
administration	
presentation	
storage	
receiving	
Hotel	15,000
Retail	10,000
Residential	10,000
Museum	5,000
School	4,400

School

	occupancy	sq.m.
Classrooms		
6 master classrooms	50	500
2 design classrooms	50	500
8 practice & test classrooms	25	400
15 classrooms for small groups	5	150
2 computer centers	50	200
Laboratories		
5 atelier spaces		100
3 labs (clothing, leather, household goods)		450
2 labs (retail, editing, publishing, phorography)		600
Library	100	300
Great Hall		700
Offices & Mobile Workstations		400
Total		4300

Museum

	sq.m.
Galleries (4 @ 700 sq.m. each)	2,800
Project Space	
Cinema	300
Internet Access/Area	
Digital Lab	300
Technical Lab	
Learning Lab	100
Library	300
Bookstore	200
Cafe & Restaurant	1,000
Storage & Preparation	
Loading Dock & Receiving	
Offices	
Total	5000+

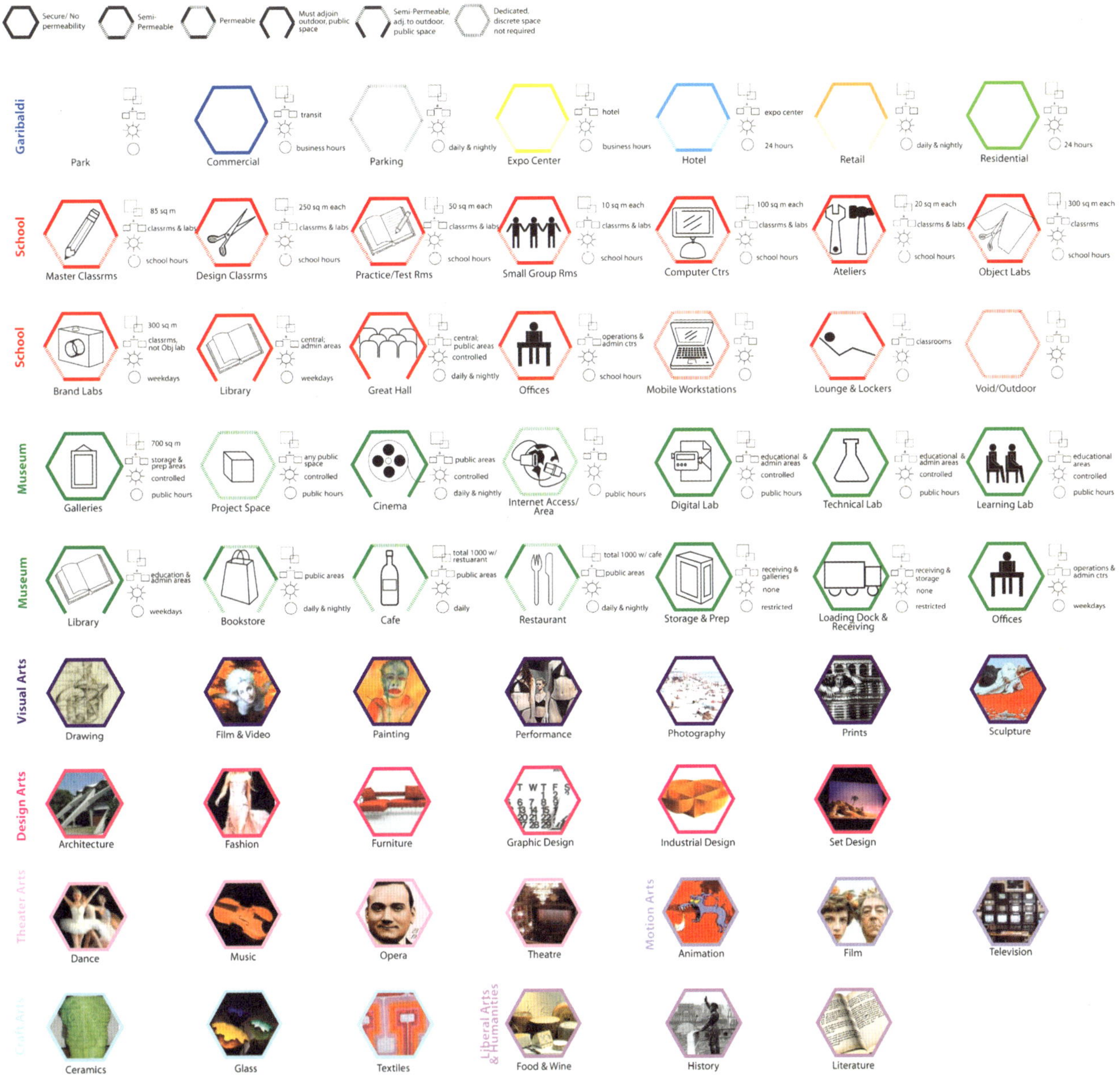

Secure/ No permeability · Semi-Permeable · Permeable · Must adjoin outdoor, public space · Semi-Permeable, adj. to outdoor, public space · Dedicated, discrete space not required

Garibaldi

Park · Commercial (transit, business hours) · Parking (daily & nightly) · Expo Center (hotel, business hours) · Hotel (expo center, 24 hours) · Retail (daily & nightly) · Residential (24 hours)

School

Master Classrms (85 sq m, classrms & labs, school hours) · Design Classrms (250 sq m each, classrms & labs, school hours) · Practice/Test Rms (50 sq m each, classrms & labs, school hours) · Small Group Rms (10 sq m each, classrms & labs, school hours) · Computer Ctrs (100 sq m each, classrms & labs, school hours) · Ateliers (20 sq m each, classrms & labs, school hours) · Object Labs (300 sq m each, classrms, school hours)

School

Brand Labs (300 sq m, classrms, not Obj lab, weekdays) · Library (central; admin areas, weekdays) · Great Hall (central; public areas, controlled, daily & nightly) · Offices (operations & admin ctrs, school hours) · Mobile Workstations · Lounge & Lockers (classrooms) · Void/Outdoor

Museum

Galleries (700 sq m, storage & prep areas, controlled, public hours) · Project Space (any public space, controlled, public hours) · Cinema (public areas, controlled, daily & nightly) · Internet Access/ Area (public hours) · Digital Lab (educational & admin areas, controlled, public hours) · Technical Lab (educational & admin areas, controlled, public hours) · Learning Lab (educational areas, controlled, public hours)

Museum

Library (education & admin areas, weekdays) · Bookstore (public areas, daily & nightly) · Cafe (total 1000 w/ restaurant, public areas, daily) · Restaurant (total 1000 w/ cafe, public areas, daily & nightly) · Storage & Prep (receiving & galleries, none, restricted) · Loading Dock & Receiving (receiving & storage, none, restricted) · Offices (operations & admin ctrs, weekdays)

Visual Arts

Drawing

Film & Video · Painting · Performance · Photography

Prints

Sculpture

Design Arts

Architecture · Fashion · Furniture · Graphic Design

Industrial Design

Set Design

Theater Arts

Dance

Music · Opera · Theatre

Motion Arts

Animation

Film

Television

Craft Arts

Ceramics

Glass

Textiles

Liberal Arts & Humanities

Food & Wine

History

Literature

Program elements: School

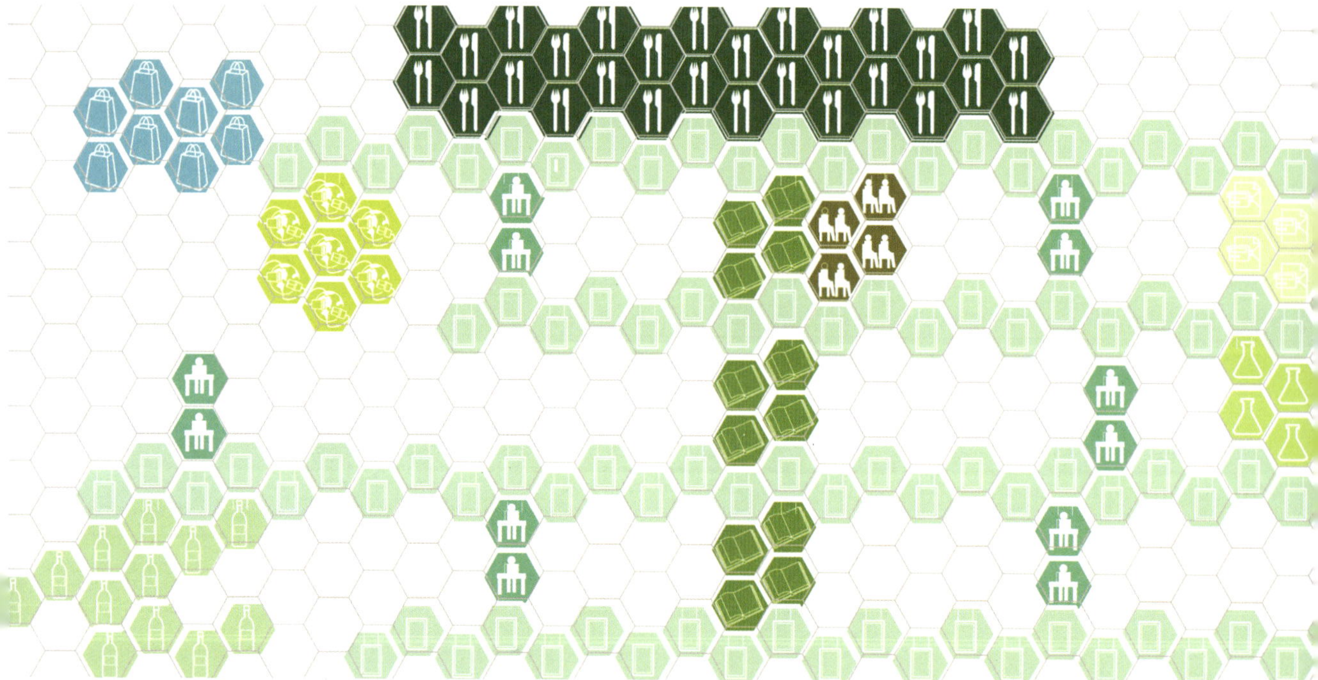

Program elements: Museum

1 ⬡ = 25 sq. m.

II. GARIBAL
REPUBBLIC
FOUNDATIC
FASHION IN
MILAN (MOI

DI GARIBALI
REPUBLIC
THE FOUND
FASHION IN
MILAN (MOI

Garibaldi Repubblica The 87-acre site in central Milan is currently the focus of one of the largest urban redevelopment initiatives in the history of the city. For nearly fifty years, the site lay vacant, although it is less than one mile from the historic center of Milan and directly adjacent to a regional center of commerce and government. The site is on the northern edge of the most central ring road, which follows the boundary of the seventeenth-century fortifications of the city. By the nineteenth century, nearly the entire city of Milan was still within these fortifications, leaving the area of Garibaldi Repubblica free for the construction of a regional rail terminus with a direct link to the main international train station on Piazza della Repubblica.

A complex set of issues—fragmented land ownership, the construction of two metro lines beneath the property, and a conservative urban planning climate—prevented any positive action until the mid-1990s, when Milan launched a redevelopment master-plan competition won by Pierluigi Nicolin. The new master plan divided the site into three bands: U1, nearest to the city center, would be a private 1.15 million-square-foot commercial mixed-use development, the *Citta della Moda* (City of Fashion); U2, in the middle, would be a large public park, *La Biblioteca degli Alberi* (Library of Trees); and U3, at the top, a government headquarters, *il Polo Instituzionale* (Institutional Center). In 2003, the Hines office in Italy, led by Riccardo Catella, assembled ownership of enough land to take control of the U1 commercial zone.

Many of the qualities that prevented development of Garibaldi Repubblica are now its primary assets. The concentration of infrastructure on the site, for one, requires a significant capital investment but also constitutes a primary advantage of the project for potential tenants. Moreover, the lack of development over the past forty years has now created a demand for contemporary class-A buildings.

Garibaldi Repubblica is a project without precedent in the modern history of Milan and requires the coordination of complex infrastructure (railways, subway, tramlines, streets, and a main outlet road to Malpensa Airport) with the interests of a speculative commercial development and the city's ambitious goal for a new urban district for leisure, culture, and fashion.

opposite: Milan in 1881, from Baedeker's Switzerland guidebook, published 1881. Site of the Garibaldi Repubblica train station is adjacent to the Porta Nuova on the northern edge of the map.

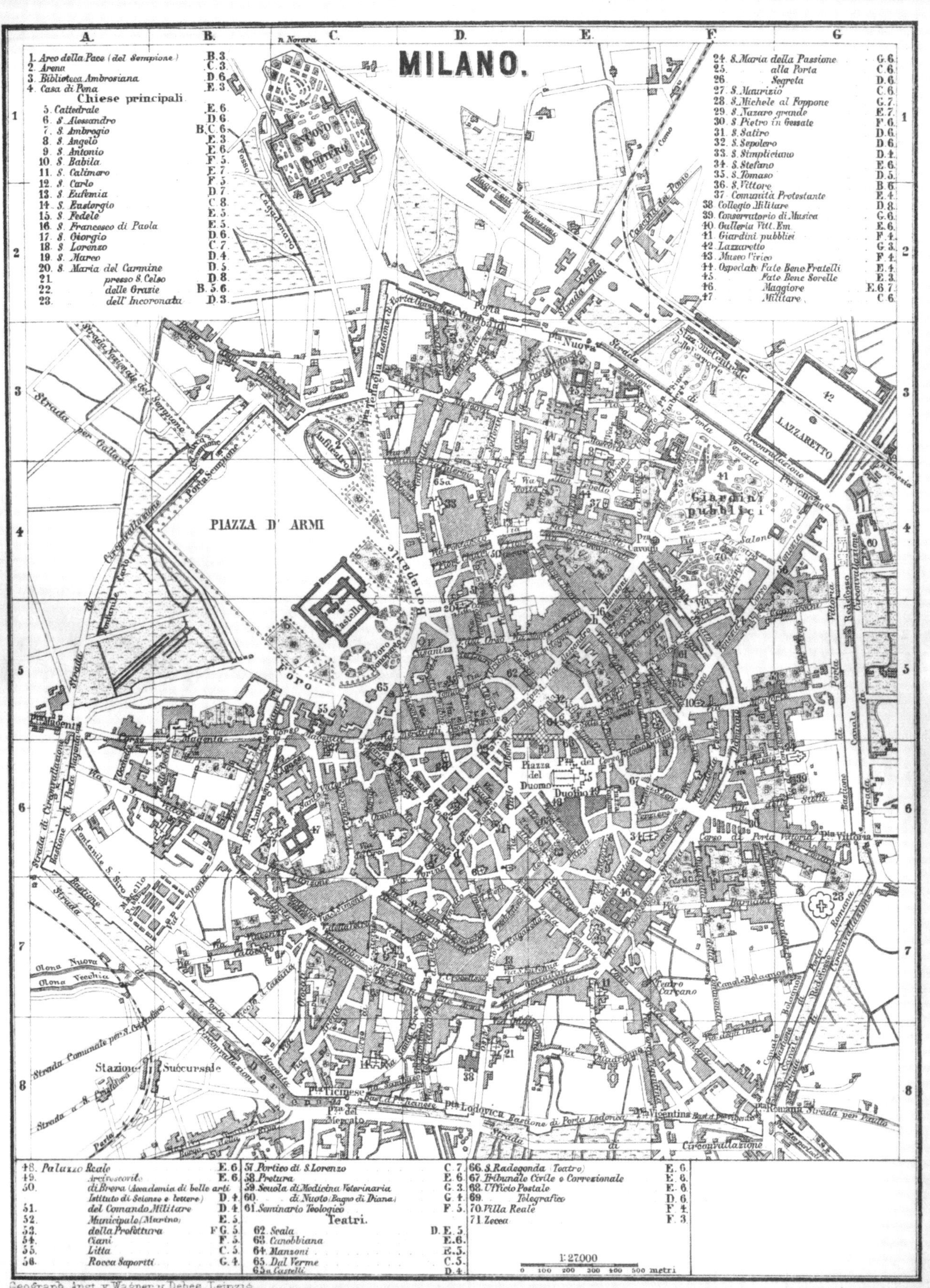

MILANO.
A. B. C. D. E. F. G
1 2 3 4 5 6 7 8
1. Arco della Pace (del Sempione) B. 3
2. Arena C. 3
3. Biblioteca Ambrosiana D. 6
4. Casa di Pena E. 3
Chiese principali
5. Cattedrale E. 6
6. S. Alessandro D. 6
7. S. Ambrogio B. C. 6
8. S. Angelo E. 3
9. S. Antonio E. 6
10. S. Babila F. 5
11. S. Calimero F. 7
12. S. Carlo F. 5
13. S. Eufemia D. 7
14. S. Eustorgio C. 8
15. S. Fedele E. 5
16. S. Francesco di Paola E. 5
17. S. Giorgio D. 6
18. S. Lorenzo C. 7
19. S. Marco D. 4
20. S. Maria del Carmine D. 5
21. presso S. Celso D. 8
22. delle Grazie B. 5. 6
23. dell' Incoronata D. 3
24. S. Maria della Passione G. 6
25. alla Porta C. 6
26. Segreta D. 6
27. S. Maurizio C. 6
28. S. Michele al Foppone G. 7
29. S. Nazaro grande E. 7
30. S. Pietro in Gessate F. 6
31. S. Satiro D. 6
32. S. Sepolcro D. 6
33. S. Simpliciano D. 4
34. S. Stefano E. 6
35. S. Tomaso D. 5
36. S. Vittore B. 6
37. Comunità Protestante E. 4
38. Collegio Militare D. 8
39. Conservatorio di Musica G. 6
40. Galleria Vitt. Em. E. 6
41. Giardini pubblici F. 4
42. Lazzaretto G. 3
43. Museo Civico F. 4
44. Ospedale Fate Bene Fratelli E. 4
45. Fate Bene Sorelle E. 3
46. Maggiore E. 6 7
47. Militare C. 6
48. Palazzo Reale E. 6
49. Arcivescovile E. 6
50. di Brera (Academia di belle arti Istituto di Scienze e lettere) D. 4
51. del Comando Militare D. 4
52. Municipale (Marino) E. 5
53. della Prefettura F. G. 5
54. Ciani F. 5
55. Litta C. 5
56. Rocca Saporiti G. 4
57. Portico di S. Lorenzo C. 7
58. Pretura E. 6
59. Scuola di Medicina Veterinaria G. 3
60. di Nuoto (Bagno di Diana) G. 4
61. Seminario Teologico F. 5
Teatri.
62. Scala D. E. 5
63. Canobbiana E. 6
64. Manzoni E. 5
65. Dal Verme C. 5
65a. Castelli D. 4
66. S. Radegonda (Teatro) E. 6
67. Tribunale Civile e Correzionale E. 6
68. Ufficio Postale E. 6
69. Telegrafico D. 6
70. Villa Reale F. 4
71. Zecca F. 3
PIAZZA D' ARMI
Castello
Foro Bonaparte
Piazza del Duomo
Giardini pubblici
LAZZARETTO
Cimitero
Arena
Pta. Nuova
Porta Garibaldi
Porta Venezia
Porta Vittoria
Porta Romana
Pta. Vigentina
Pta. Lodovica
Pta. Ticinese
Pta. Magenta
Porta Sempione
Stazione Succursale
Olona Nuova
Olona Vecchia
Teatro Carcano
Strada per Gallarate
Strada per Pavia
Strada per Paullo
n. Novara
Como
1: 27000
0 100 200 300 400 500 metri
Geograph. Anst. v. Wagner u. Debes, Leipzig.

MEDIOL
Porta Vercellina
S. Nicolo
Porta Ticinese
And. Alc Des armes
de ceste Ville
de Milon
L'enfant naissāt d'un Serpent par la bouche
De son clair Sang les nobles armes touche,
Nous auons veu d'Alexandre Monarque
Pour s'annoblir, monnoye à belle marque
Quand fils d'Ammon sous forme Serpētine
Se dict conceu par Semence diuine
On dict Serpens par bouche Serpenter:
Née est Pallas du cerueau de Jupiter.

VM
Porta Comaña
Porta Noua
Porta Orietale
Porta Tonsa
Grego rio
MEDIOLANVM Metropolis Insubrum, vulgò Mila:
no, vrbs potentiæ & dignitatis eximiæ, quæ ob præstante
loci commoditatē, Imperator Romanorum sedes, plerumq;
fuit, qui superbissimis eam ædificijs exornarunt. Circa quam
nobilis regio tum coeli temperie, tum soli fertilitate, et afflu:
enti rerum copia, vnde ciuitas suo abundans populo, et pro:
prijs nitens viribus, semper gentis fuit caput, et quotiens
euersa, post excidium restituta, vbertate agri, et propin:
quitate Alpium, ex quibus hominum copia affluit. Ingē:
ti incremento res Mediolanensis tempore Gratiani Cæsaris
aucta erat. Nā quingentos et amplius annos, neq; ab externo hos
te, nec intestino bello Insubres vexati fuère. Durauit illa foe:
licitas vsq; ad D. Ambrosij tēpora, quib9 Arriana heresis.
maximis calamitatib9 hanc vrbē affecit. Deinde Attila in Ita
liā ingress9 Mediolanum diruit, Instauratū, aliquāto tē:
pore quieuit. Mox à Longobardis maximis agitatur moles:
tijs, Quib9 à Carolo Magno domitis, ānos trecētos et sexagīta floru:
it. Deīde verò Fridericus Barbarossa Mediolanū solo æquauit.
Cuius incolę tandē Parmensiū et Placentinor; ope, tanto ani:
mor; ardore patriā restaurarūt, vt multo quam ante ditior,
potētior, frequentiorq; extiterit. Quod sanè maximā huius
vrbis potentiā arguit, quod post tam frequētes hostiū di:
reptiones, in tantā magnitudinem rursus excreuerit.
CVM PRIVILEGIO.

The City: Gianni Verga, Comune di Milano In a discussion with Gianni Verga, the students learned about the numerous development schemes in Milan and the history of the Garibaldi Repubblica project.

Milan currently has more development projects under way than at any point in the last forty years. Much of the activity is the result of a new master plan prepared in the 1990s that identified the need for a comprehensive transformation of urban planning practice in the city and then specified two major axes for new development as indicated on the *carta delle politiche urbanistiche*—one running from the commercial center near Malpensa in the northwest to the residential areas in the southeast and another running from the Nuova Fiera di Milano to the historic center of the city at the Duomo.

Nearly all of the major projects under construction in Milano fall somewhere along these two axes. Garibaldi Repubblica, at their intersection, includes the Hines-Pelli project, a large public park by Petra Blaisse and Michael Maltzan, and a new headquarters for the Lombardi regional government by Pei Cobb Freed and Partners. At the southeast edge, near Linate airport, is the Santa Giulia project by Norman Foster, which combines housing, offices, shops, restaurants, and cafés with cultural facilities such as a Congress Center and Exhibition Hall, as well as generous green spaces and a large central park on a 275-acre site, making this the largest project currently in development. At the north is Bicocca, completed in 2004, which includes a new university campus and substantial residential development. Nearby is the Nuova Fiera by Massimiliano Fuksas, a 7.5 million-square-foot convention center which opened in late 2005. There is also a major mixed-use project in the planning stage for the old Fiera in central Milan that includes offices towers by Zaha Hadid, Daniel Libeskind, and Arata Isozaki, as well as a residential, cultural, and retail component. The department of urban planning in Milan has also begun to plan the reuse of nearly 2,000 acres of abandoned industrial area, which will be the future center of the ongoing transformation of the city.

previous: Georg Braun and Frans Hogenberg's map of Milan, 1572, after a print made ca.1560 by Antonio Lafreri.

opposite top: *Carta delle trasformazioni* (Map of Architectural Projects in Milan). Courtesy of the Urban Center, Comune di Milano, 2005.

opposite bottom: *Carta delle politiche urbanistiche* (Regional Master Plan for Milan). Courtesy of the Urban Center, Comune di Milano, 2005. Note the position of Garibaldi Repubblica at the intersection of the two axes.

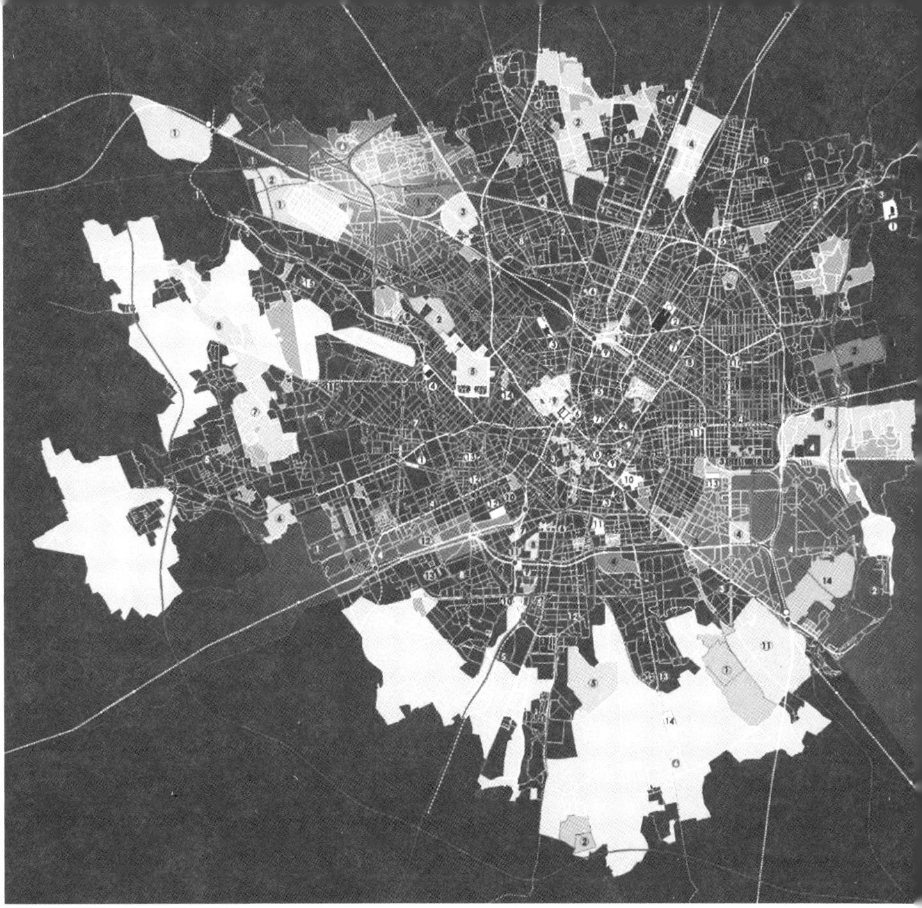

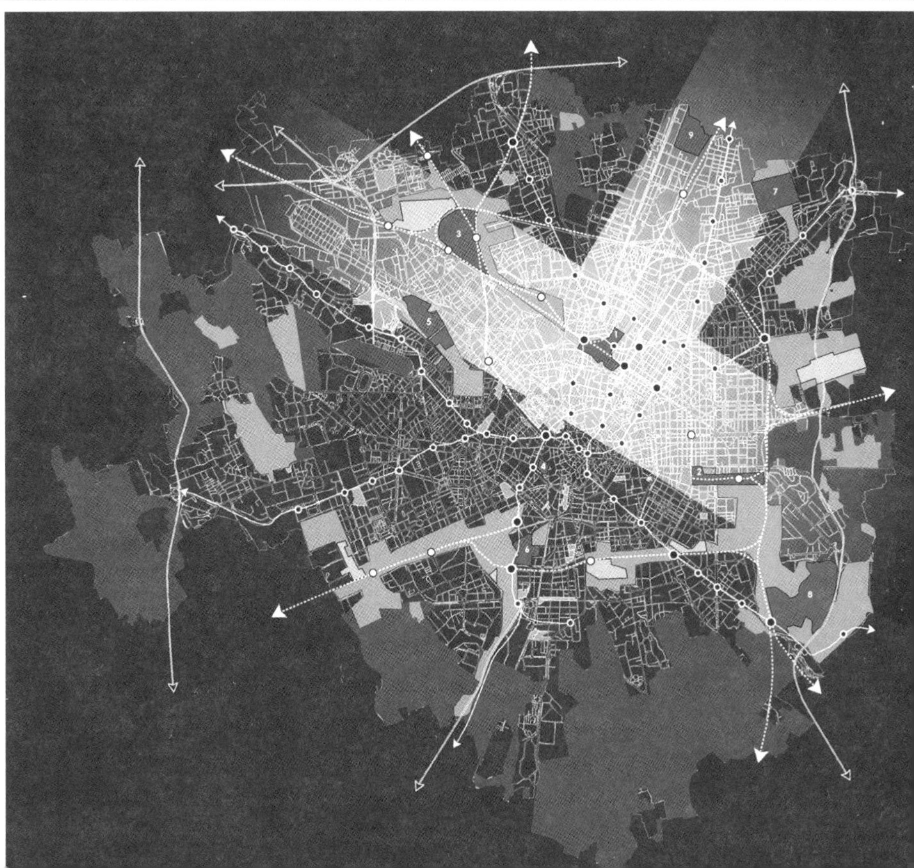

Q: Why are all these projects going up now, in Milan, seemingly all at once?

GV: Milan has suffered from a long period of immobility due to a very rigid city master plan. This period dated from the 1970s to the 1990s, and only recently with new urban planning practices has the city been able to become more dynamic.

Q: What is the expected impact of the new Fiera di Milano?

GV: The real cultural value of this project is its ability to open certain actives inside the Fiera to the outside world that previously have been off-limits to the majority of the population in Milan. So there will be a large change in the character of the Fiera: from a closed institution to a very open place, made possible in large part by Fuksas' building. In addition, there will be a museum of design, which was proposed by the developers. This is design in the most inclusive sense of the term, and the museum will be different from the museum of fashion at Garibaldi Repubblica.

The new exhibition hall will be the biggest exhibition center in the world and will keep alive the Milanese tradition of large exhibition events, which has been a main part of the city's life and economy since the 1950s.

Q: What sort of spillover effect do you expect around the Fiera?

GV: The idea, of course, is to have the Fiera start a process of general development, but you have to remember that the Fiera is an important strategic venue not just for Milan and the local surrounding areas but also for a very important economic corridor that goes from Lisbon to Madrid to Milan, then farther down to Kiev. The Fiera will be part of this system that integrates local issues and much more international issues.

opposite top: Norman Foster and Partners, Santa Giulia, 2003. Site: 271 acres (housing, office, retail, public park).

opposite middle: Daniel Libeskind, Zaha Hadid, Arata Isozaki, and Pier Paolo Maggiora, Fiera Milano, competition 2004, project completion 2012. Site area: 2,750,000 sq. ft. (office, housing, cultural).

opposite bottom: Massimiliano Fuksas Architects, Nuovo Fiera di Milan. completed 2005. Gross building area: 2,100,000 sq. ft. (exhibition).

Q: Many of these projects in Milan appear be quite similar and have similar construction schedules. Do you think this will result in excessive competition between the projects or, perhaps, can they work to complement one another?

GV: There will be no overlap. For example, the Museum of Design in the Nuova Fiera is totally different from the Museum of Fashion, MOdAM, at Garibaldi Repubblica. In addition, you must remember that Milan is very late in providing these types of facilities and services. So now, what may look like competition is really just projects that are filling up a gap to reach the normal level of other metropolitan cities in the world.

Q: We understand that the city has been very specific in terms of the guidelines it set for the Garibaldi Repubblica project, specifically limits to the uses permitted and acceptable floor areas for those uses. Can you give us a sense of how the city set these sort of limits?

GV: First of all, the specifications for any single development always refer to a much more general framework that established the aims and future guidelines for the new developments in Milan. One of them, for instance, was emphasis on green areas. Another one was emphasis on bringing back residential to the city, with a particular aim to build more social housing. The third major strategy was to provide student housing in the city, for which there is currently a huge need. And within this general framework the municipality identified areas of excellent potential, where the vocation of the site, if you will, was in line with a certain aim of the overall framework. At Garibaldi Repubblica, for instance, we saw potential with fashion, so we are planning for a Citta della Moda. For Bicocca, on the other hand, the potential was with education, so the center of the project is the new university campus. At Santa Giulia, the potential was residential, so the emphasis in the planning guidelines is intended to stimulate residential development. So these are the general rules that are guiding the urban development of Milan.

Q: In our initial research, we learned about the changing demographics of Italy in general and Milan in particular. For example, most major cities are currently contracting as the population as a whole is getting significantly older. I am curious if the current development could be seen as a strategy to address these changes in Milan?

GV: Yes, it can, in a sense. One of the trends we have observed is that the city was losing inhabitants, so in our current planning we placed an emphasis on bringing back residents to the core of the city. For example, the municipality of Milano has made available 1.7 million square meters of space for residential development, both for open-market and subsidized housing in the last few years.

Q: For Garibaldi Repubblica, what is goal for the new transportation infrastructure in the project?

GV: The Garibaldi Repubblica has the highest density of infrastructure for all of northern Italy. We expect the majority of visitors to arrive by public transportation. So this is the first priority. On the other hand, we are also building a new road system that passes through the project, which will allow people to travel from the center of the city to the outskirts in a very short amount of time.

—Translation: Carlo Matta

above and next page: Existing conditions in early 2005 at Garibaldi Repubblica, with the Stazione Garibaldi and the Corso Como neighborhood.

The Client: Beatrice Trussardi, Foundation of Fashion Trussardi is the president and chief executive officer of Trussardi Group, one of the most prominent MADE IN ITALY fashion and luxury brands in the world. She is also president of the Foundazione Nicola Trussardi, a nonprofit institute for contemporary art and culture, as well as vice president for the Fondazione della Moda, Design, Communicazione in Milan (the Foundation of Fashion, Design, and Communication). Trussardi joined the Fondazione della Moda in 2003 and with its president, Gabriele Albertini, the mayor of Milan, has been responsible for organizing MOdAM. The students and professors met with Trussardi in Milan and asked her questions about the program of the foundation and MOdAM.

Milan, 2005
Beatrice Trussardi: The Foundation of Fashion was born four years ago with the mission to establish the guidelines for the Garibaldi Repubblica project, in particular the nonprofit component, MOdAM, which includes the fashion museum and school. At the beginning, the main question for the foundation was, What kind of nonprofit do we need in Milan for fashion? Our conclusion was that it should be a new kind of design museum. It should not have a permanent collection but instead be a place for research, for pursuing a range of disciplines, from fashion to art to photography, design, and so on. It should be a center of research and study, and that is why we decided there should also be an educational facility.

In terms of the content of the museum, we were thinking about a contemporary place. So we feel the museum should not be focused on a traditional archive. It should not, for example, be like the Costume Institute at the Metropolitan Museum of Art, in New York. Instead, we explored other ways of thinking about what a museum collection can be. For instance, we have considered establishing a virtual archive that would be collected from existing archives at the fashion houses. Armani, let's say, who has a very large archive, can become a virtual part of the museum, allowing the curators at MOdAM to access his archive for use in exhibitions. Flexible, multi-use open space, for a wide range of different exhibitions that can vary from time to time, will also a very important feature of the new building.

opposite and page 079: Behnisch Hines Yale studio visit to Garibaldi Repubblica site and city of Milan.

LOUIS VUITTON
PRADA
PRADA
PRADA

The center of this building, we felt, should be the university. Although we are talking about two different nonprofit programs—a school and a museum—we would prefer to see the two integrated into a single building. We like to think of this like a piece of fruit: the center, the pit, as the school and around it, the museum and exhibition space.

The museum has been named MOdAM, which is a linkage of "modern" and "fashion." We chose this name because we think the museum should be the connector between all the different elements in the project and in Milan.

The MOdAM museum will include six parts: The first part, "ante-MOdAM," will organize exhibitions around Milan before the actual building is finished. These should be experimental, daring, and should serve to introduce MOdAM to the public and the city. The "Subject-Project" will present a series of conventional exhibitions, each focused on a specific theme. Students in the school will have the opportunity to be involved with the production of these exhibitions and follow the production from beginning to the end. "Logos/Places" will explore projects about the relationship between fashion media and contemporary communications technology. The fourth element, "Melting Space," will concentrate on collaborations between different media, including art, photography, design, architecture, and fashion. In this area we can work on the creation of new, independent works either inside or outside the context of fashion. "MOdAM-Global" will focus on research of the international fashion industry and culture. Finally, "MOdAM Production" will be a center for the production of dance and theater performance as well as cinema, video, and music. It will involve choreographers, directors, designers, and artists and will create new projects that will be presented first in Milan and then travel to other similar museums around the world.

The MOdAM school will be a collaboration between three universities in Milan: Università Bocconi, for economics and business management; Politechnico for design; and Università Cattolica, which concentrates on the social sciences. Each university already has an established curriculum and faculty. At MOdAM, the three will come together and produce a new interdisciplinary program for fashion and fashion management. This will be a very important step for the fashion industry in Italy.

The building will be a very important part of this. The two buildings will have different technical requirements, as Hines has provided, but we also want the two buildings to come together. The museum is for the public, and at the same time we want the students to be a full part of MOdAM—not just working in the same building but real players in MOdAM, together with the curators and the staff of the museum. The buildings should be the same. Synergy between museum and school is the goal.

The mission of MOdAM is to create not just a new institution, but a system with both a national and international purview. By bringing together different media and culture, we hope to create some synergy—new connections, new energy. This should be a place for real contemporary culture in Milan. Now, we don't have any contemporary museums in Milan. This should be the one.

Q: What is your vision for the role of the fashion industry in the Citta della Moda?

BT: I think it shouldn't be considered a ghetto for fashion. It shouldn't be a district in the sense that all the fashion houses move there and just fashion will be there. Fashion is a connector. Fashion and design are the most important things in Italian industry. So fashion can include every other type of business and other sorts of creative things, but Garibaldi Repubblica shouldn't be only focused on fashion. The entire atmosphere of the entire project should be inspired by MOdAM. This is some matter of concern. We cannot try to become another Via Monte Napoleone or a place where everyone has a showroom or office. This should be a new center of Milan: very creative, very eclectic, very vital. It should be alive twenty-four hours a day. It shouldn't be like a shopping street. If you go to Via Monte Napoleone after 7 p.m., nobody is around, there are no restaurants or bars. This should be different.

Q: Can you explain more about the character or the image of the museum that you hope to create?

BT: It should express that fashion is inspired by everything around us and inspires everything in turn. And the kind of exhibitions at MOdAM should reflect this—the exchange between fashion and our contemporary life. It is not just about clothes, a way of wearing clothes. It is an attitude, a way of living. Fashion inspires everything today—image, advertising—and these kinds of things are inspirations for our lives. MOdAM should express this complexity, but if you think about it, it's very simple. It is obvious today.

Q: Who do you expect will be coming to visit MOdAM?

BT: We expect all different kinds of people: Students, artists, young people, men, women, industry, intellectuals, politicians, cultural operators, fashion victims, architects, journalists, everyone who is usually in Milan. Most foreigners think that the most beautiful city in Italy is either Florence or Rome, but actually Milan has the greatest number of tourists each year. But these tourists most of the time are here for work, not just for leisure. There is a lot of traffic from international people, creative types—very interactive, very international people here. We have fashion, we have design, so the public should be very broad. The most-visited museums in Italy are the Uffizi in Florence, Citta Vaticana in Rome—the ancient museums—but we don't have a good contemporary space.

Q: In what way will the school embody what you consider to be essential to Italian fashion?

BT: Italian fashion is larger than the brand, because it is supported by industry. MADE IN ITALY is very important because the designers themselves, like Valentino, are very connected to the manufacturing base that produces the clothes. But now there is a big change, because, as you know, China and India are replacing Italian production. As a result, many Italian industries are failing in the face of new competition. What is so important about MOdAM and also what makes fashion in general so important in Milan, more important than the industry in Paris or New York, is that here it is not just a matter of design but of a national manufacturing enterprise, a whole way of life.

MAX&Co.

The Master Plan: Pelli Clarke Pelli Hines selected Pelli Clarke Pelli as the master-plan architects for the Garibaldi Repubblica project after a competition in spring 2002. The current master plan was finalized in 2004 and obtained approval from the municipality in Milan in 2005. Cesar Pelli is a former dean of the Yale School of Architecture (1977–1984) and established his New Haven-based architectural practice in 1977. In 1995, the American Institute of Architects awarded Cesar Pelli its Gold Medal. Cesar Pelli is the author of *Observations for Young Architects* (The Monacelli Press, 1999), a reflection on the practice and the method of architecture.

Cesar Pelli was a member of the midterm and final studio reviews and also offered these observations to the students about the actual project and the studio project.

New Haven, 2005
The Garibaldi Repubblica site in Milan was not an appealing site because it has no edge. By "no edge" I mean, there is nothing of much interest on its periphery that you would like to relate to. At the north, what you see today is not at all what will be there after the design is done. And toward the south, it is rather uninteresting. The most interesting thing there, and we made much of it, is the Corso Como, and bringing the Corso into the project was very important. You also have the Stazione Garibaldi, which is heavily used but quite a poor building.

You are in Milan but you are not in Milan, because there is no Milan continuity. But one is still in Milan. This will be inhabited and used by Milanese, and they will come with their ideas and expectations.

A basic problem in the master plan design was, how do you build over all the infrastructure, including the railway, metro lines and station, and the Via della Liberazione? This was the foundation of our scheme. In the competition, we competed with Norman Foster and an Italian architect, but I believe we were the only ones to solve the problem of the infrastructure, and that was the key. Once you solve that problem, it sets up a series of design decisions that carry you to an architectural strategy.

opposite: Major development sites in Milan.

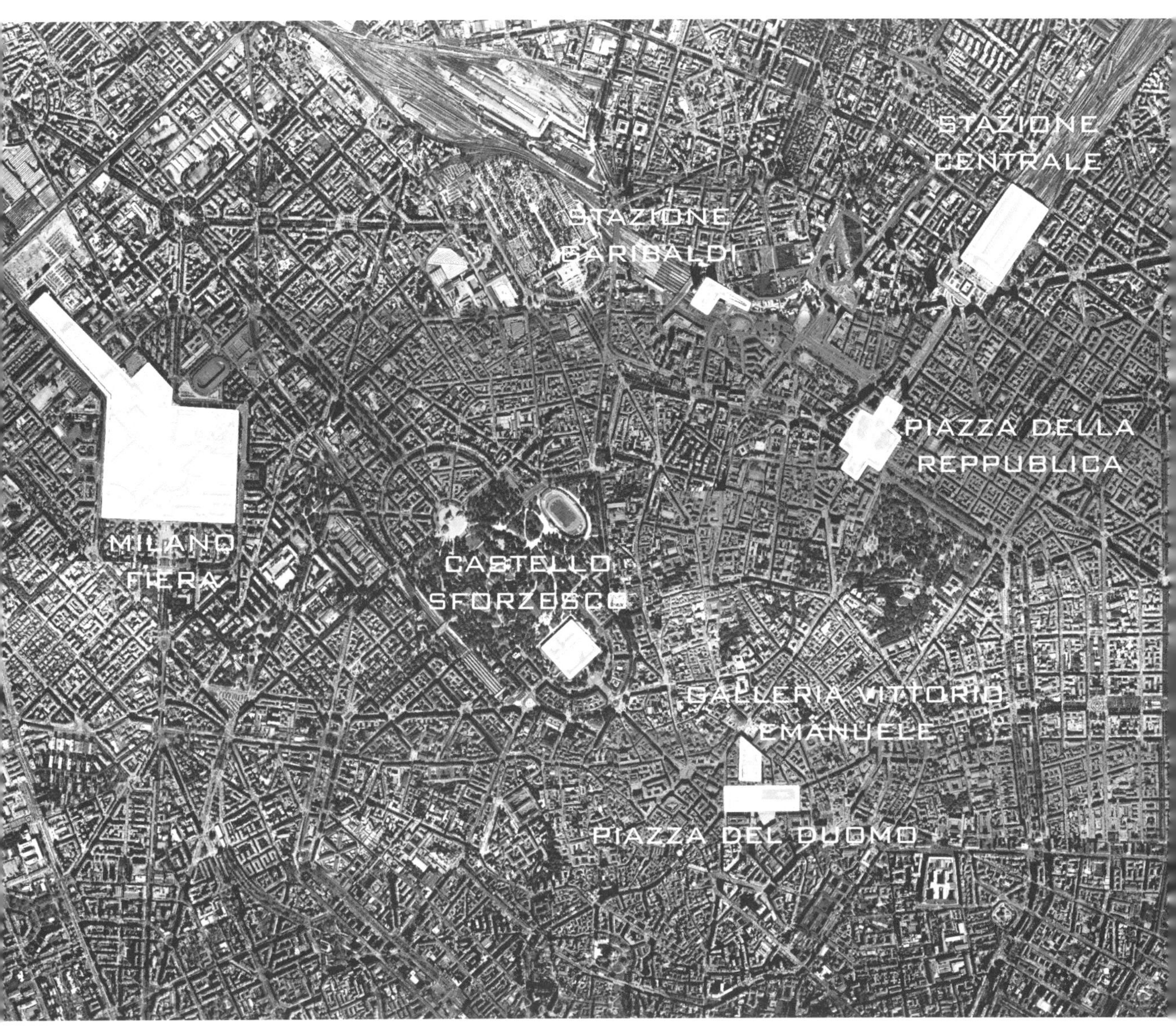
STAZIONE
CENTRALE
STAZIONE
GARIBALDI
PIAZZA DELLA
REPPUBLICA
MILANO
FIERA
CASTELLO
SFORZESCO
GALLERIA VITTORIO
EMANUELE
PIAZZA DEL DUOMO

opposite: Pelli Clarke Pelli Master Plan. Filling the void at Garibaldi Repubblica will force the union of three very different neighborhoods with no historic connection to one another: At the north of the site is the Isola, home to the working class and base of leftist politics in Milan; to the south is Corso Como, full of restaurants, nightclubs, and the fashion industry; all of the other buildings are owned by the government, including the Pirelli Building by Gio Ponti and Pier Luigi Nervi. Bisecting the site is Via del Nord, a highway that leads to the northern suburbs. At the west is the Stazione Garibaldi, an international and commuter rail station with a capacity for over 250,000 passengers a day.

above: Garibaldi Repubblica as could be fully built, showing the competition's winning park design, *La Biblioteca degli Alberi*, 2005, by INSIDE/OUTSIDE, a landscape collaborative based in the Netherlands including Petra Blaisse, Mirko Zardini, Mathias Lehner, Irma Boom, Piet Oudolf, and Michael Maltzan.

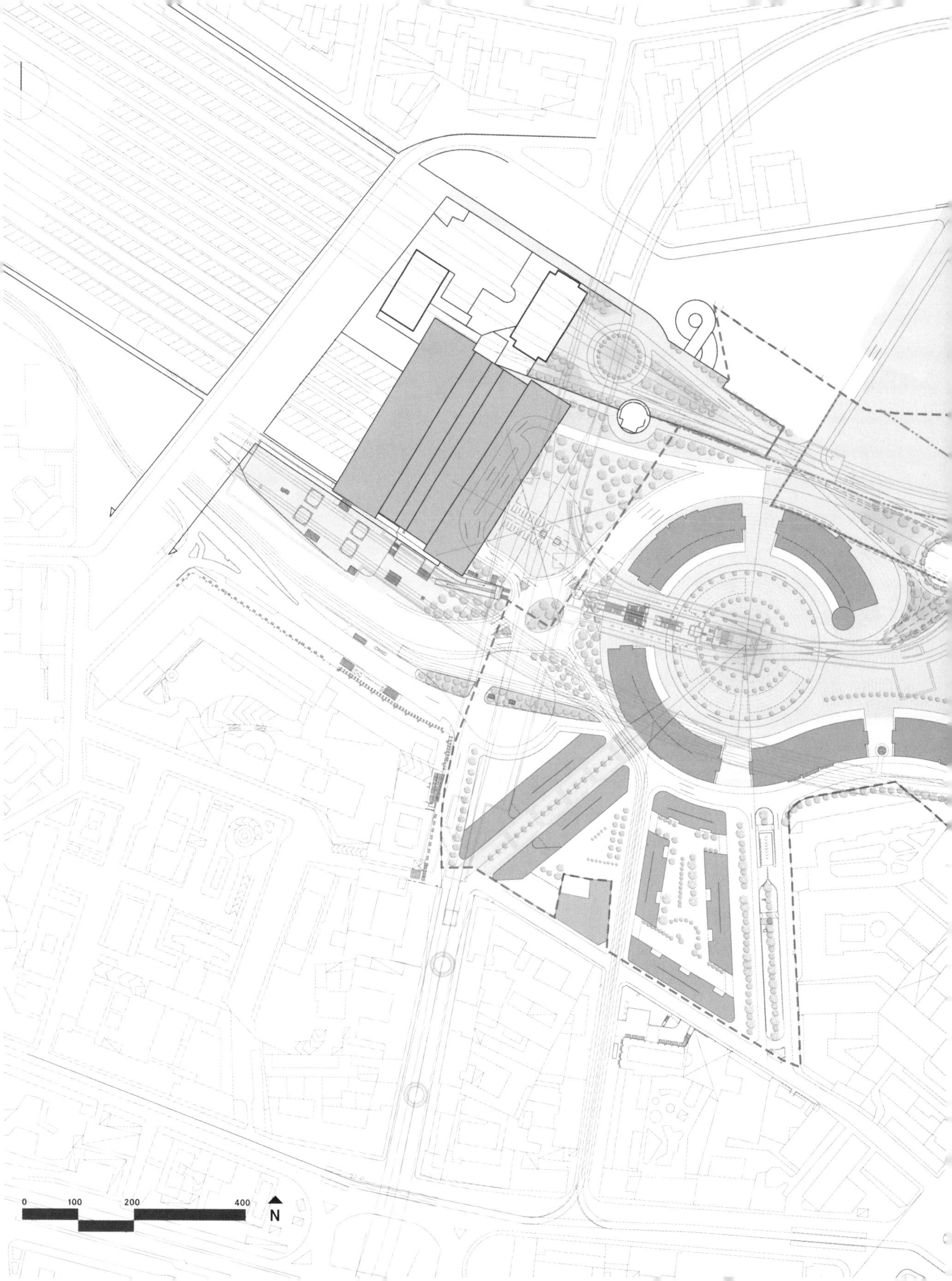

0
100
200
400
N

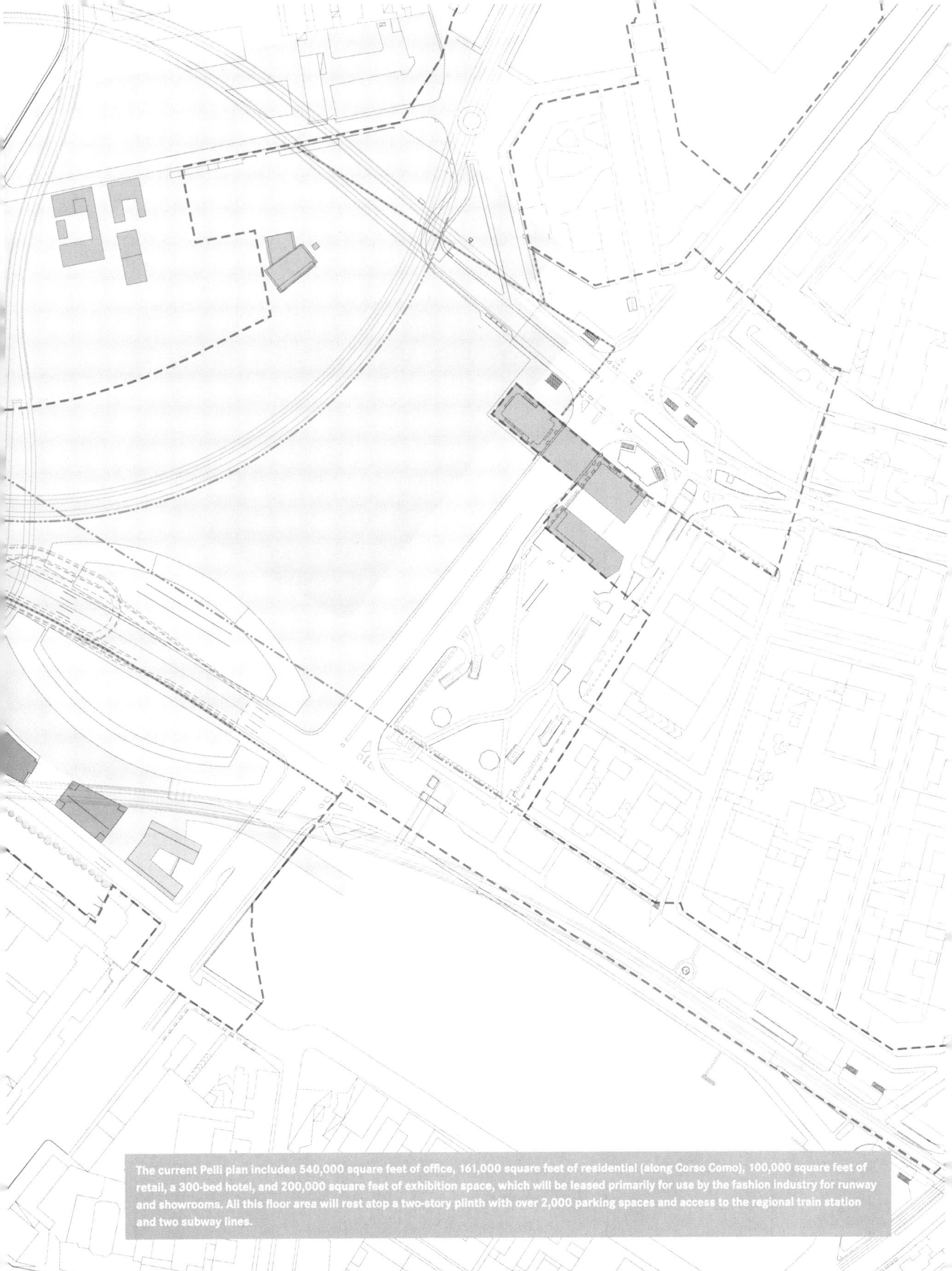

The current Pelli plan includes 540,000 square feet of office, 161,000 square feet of residential (along Corso Como), 100,000 square feet of retail, a 300-bed hotel, and 200,000 square feet of exhibition space, which will be leased primarily for use by the fashion industry for runway and showrooms. All this floor area will rest atop a two-story plinth with over 2,000 parking spaces and access to the regional train station and two subway lines.

One of the complicated parts of the infrastructure design is how to account for the rise in the rail line from the northern edge of the project, where it is below grade, to the western edge, where it is above grade. The city would like very much to create a north-south street through the project, but it can only happen if it would go above the rail line—and that would be very costly. The ramp is opposed by the neighborhood and would create more problems than it would solve. The other problem for us to solve was the large amount of traffic coming on Via della Liberazione. The city wanted to get this traffic out of the local city streets, and that's why we ended up channeling it partially under the park. Liberazione is intended to carry high-speed traffic, unlike a normal Milanese street.

For Hines, an imperative affecting the master plan was the need to park approximately 3,000 cars on the site, which cannot go below grade because of the subway lines and station, so we designed a podium. The parking will make the offices very marketable, because in Milan you rarely have parking on-site. The parking will be lined with offices and retail, so that it will be almost invisible.

An important thing to remember about this project is that there are probably more infrastructure problems here than anywhere else in northern Italy. That is the main reason why this site remained undeveloped since World War II—because it takes a huge investment to transform it into a usable site. That is why they brought in someone like Hines who is a developer of a scale (not only a scale, but a vision) that the Italians do not have yet. That is why he is able to pull it off now. He has also acquired the adjacent site, Ex. Varesine, which makes his project a truly massive investment of buildings.

These were the main issues. We had to work with the original master plan by Pierluigi Nicolin, and we worked closely with him—he was included in many of our meetings, and we listened to him very carefully. The city also had many concerns, such as the integrity of the subways and the preservation of the plan by Nicolin as well as the amount of traffic we had to accommodate on via Liberazione. Together

opposite top: City of Milan's proposed master plan by Pierluigi Nicolin. Entry in an open public competition sponsored by the city of Milan in 1991.

opposite bottom: Winning competition scheme, Biblioteca degli Alberi, by INSIDE/OUTSIDE, 2004. Landscaped area: approximately 600,000 square feet.

with the number of parking spaces we had to have for Hines, these were probably the most serious issues we had to deal with in order to start designing. This was a fairly short competition. Because of our experience, we could offer solutions to the infrastructure fairly quickly and then start designing.

In the Yale studio, what surprised me in all the reviews and discussion that I participated in is that the students never, ever questioned the developer. Nobody ever questioned Hines. It's a pity. I thought at the beginning that this would indeed be a studio about working with a developer. It would have been interesting to challenge the developer and then design, because if you would challenge him, he then will turn around and challenge you.

One important decision was the choice of MOdAM as the problem for the studio, not just one of the Hines projects. MOdAM in reality is outside of Hines' responsibility and site—the museum is meant to be in the park, public land—so it does not impinge on the commercial development in the slightest. Hines never had any reason to feel uncomfortable, because his real project was untouched by the work in the studio. In many ways, I felt the same about our design. Nobody was really looking at the problems that we had to deal with, so the students were not addressing any of the problems that we had to solve—which perhaps may have been too complicated, too difficult, to be faced by them in a semester.

If the studio had taken a piece of Hines—the master plan, one of the commercial buildings—that would have been more difficult, but the class would have gotten something from Hines. It may have been a less interesting project because all of the parts of the project that Hines will develop are not as interesting for a student as the museum. Sometimes you have to do that in school. To do a commercial project and have to adhere to the commercial needs of the developer would have been a very demanding exercise. You can become creative in commercial projects only after you have full control over the pragmatic aspects of it. You can do this after a few years of practice. Then you can concentrate on the artistic aspects.

There was something appealing about the difficulty. On the one hand, because it was a project on the scale of the city, there were several students who said, "Well, let's do urban design, at least for the first half of the semester." But the students who tried to work at that scale for the first half had a difficult time doing architecture in the second half.

Urban design and building design were separated, when they are really one and the same thing. The only way to do urban design is if you do architecture from the beginning, and the only way to do architecture is if you solve the urban design issues. But this would have been a very difficult, real problem. It was fine for a four-month studio to design a museum where you did not have to worry too much about the particularities of the site or of a museum.

Studios have focused on commercial projects in the past but always with huge elasticity, a huge grain of salt, so that they become not very different from an institutional project. There are no questions of cost or of political problems or of the market. There are many other particulars in those projects, which are very interesting but would have consumed the semester just to understand them.

next page: Pelli Clarke Pelli, Garibaldi Repubblica Master Plan, rendering of anticipated full build-out, Milan, Italy, 2004.

Yale Student Master Planning Strategies The first master plan of Garibaldi Repubblica by Pierluigi Nicolin was drawn for the city of Milan as a guide for planning and zoning decisions on the redevelopment of the site. It is more a document of public policy than of urban design. The principal goal of the plan was to establish regulations for program and use (how much and where) and to evaluate the impact of that program on existing infrastructure, leaving aside more architectural questions like massing and circulation.

The second master plan by Pelli Clarke Pelli was awarded after an architectural competition in which the participants were given the Nicolin plan and asked to revise it according to a set of functional criteria established by Hines. The challenge for this plan was to adapt the program permitted by the city to the requirement from Hines for a commercially viable development and the demands of an exceptionally complex transportation infrastructure at Garibaldi Repubblica.

As the first plan was about policy and the second about architecture and finance, the master plans from the Behnisch Hines studio at Yale approached urban design from the bottom up: first, the design of a single building, MOdAM, then the design of the urban context. The master plans from Yale extended ideas formed from architecture about circulation, infrastructure, program, and massing into the landscape and urban organization of Garibaldi Repubblica, leading to revisions or outright replacements to the Pelli Clarke Pelli plan. From a building about programmatic adjacencies came a plan about density; from a building about unbroken surfaces came a plan about landscape. There is a continuity in these projects between the urban and the architectural, a testing of ideas very small and very big.

opposite: Student project by Ceren Bingol.

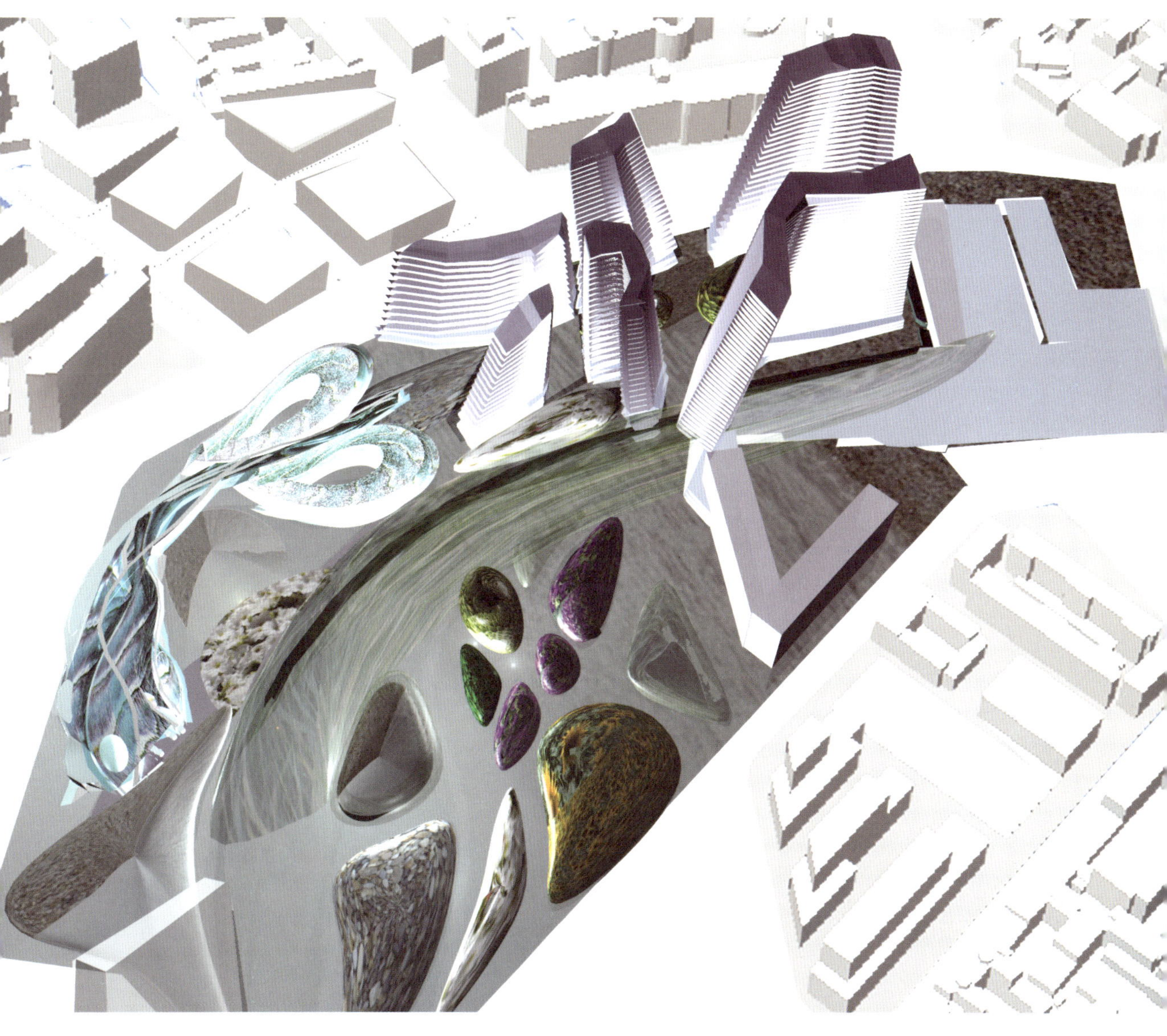

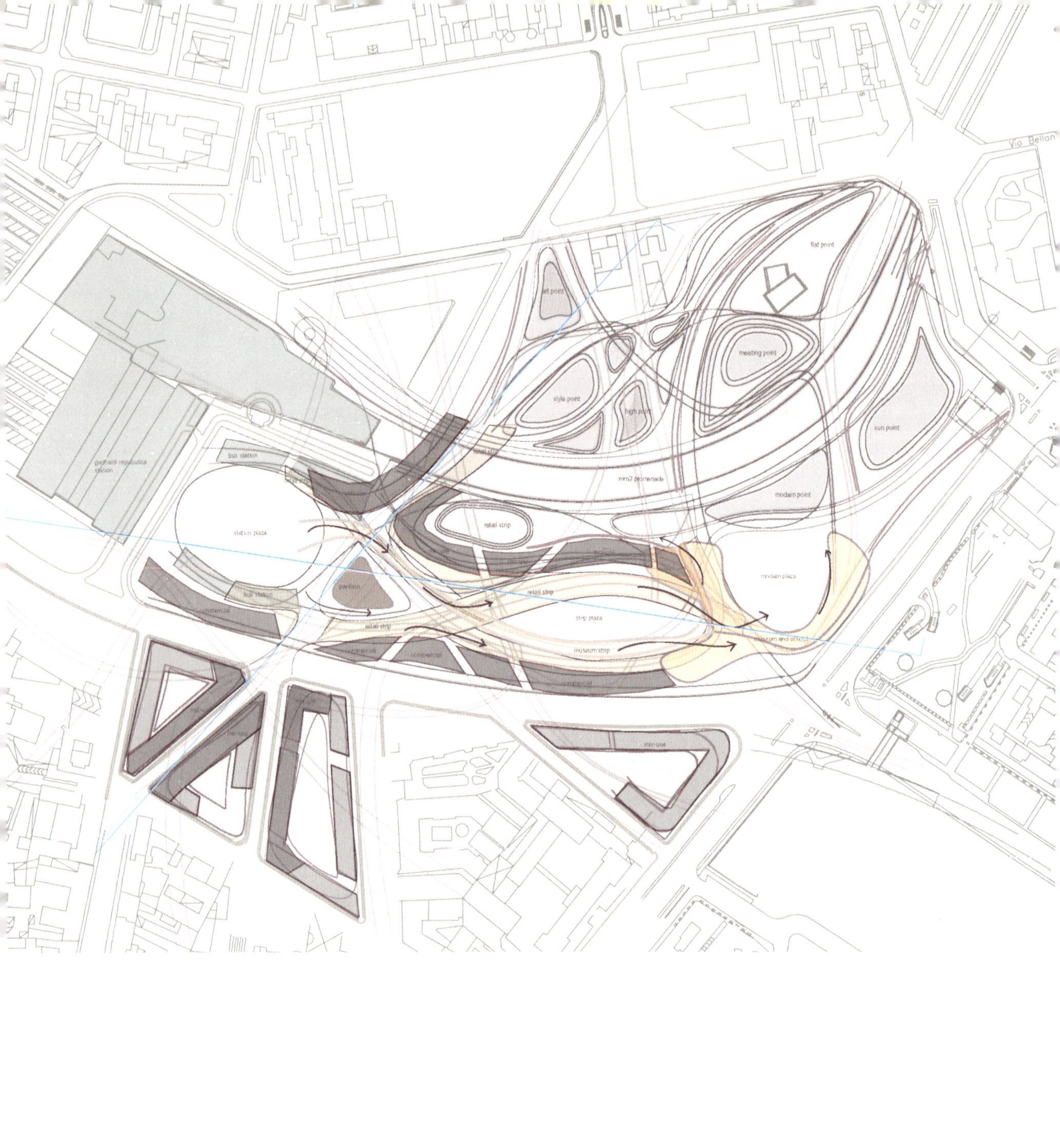

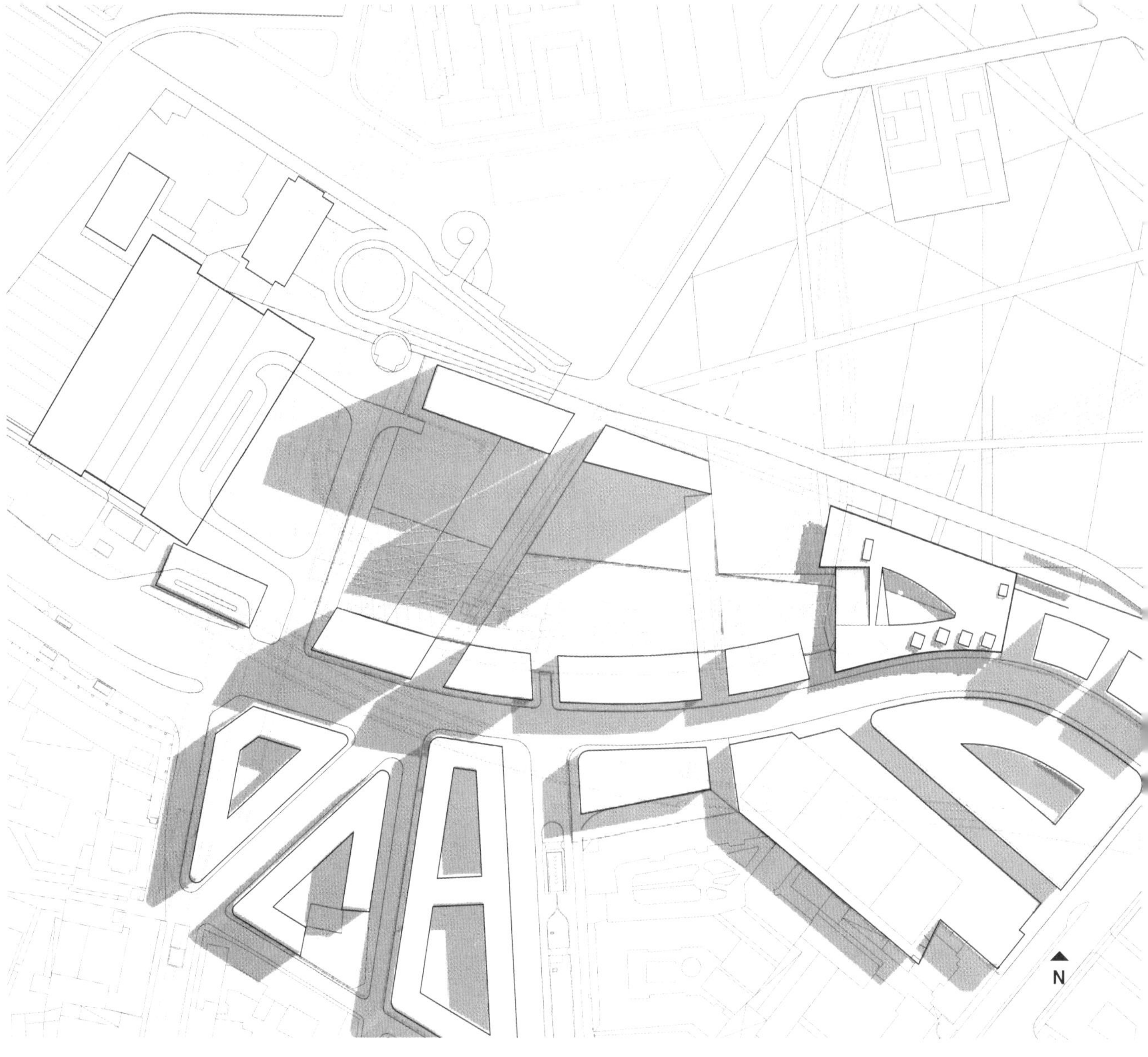

opposite: This master plan is the result of an analysis of vehicular and pedestrian circulation in the Cesar Pelli proposal. Two axes form the primary urban armature. Project by students Ceren Bingol and Jennifer Newsom. One runs north-south to connect the Corso Como entertainment district to the Isola residential neighborhood; this axis would be utilized continuously throughout the day. A second axis, for primarily daytime commercial use, runs east-west between the train station and MOdAM, fashion museum, and school. Along this axis would be an arcade with office, residential, and retail spaces.

above: In the current plan by students Genevieve Fu and Brett Spearman, the primary boulevard, Via del Nord, runs along the northern side of the project, underneath a canopy connecting the Citta della Moda to the new park and between the Stazione Garibaldi and the commercial development. This plan inverts the position of the road, from the north to the south, and through that simple gesture completely reconfigures the urban relationship between the three primary elements: park, Hines development, and station.

DEVELOPMENT CENTERS

PIAZZAS, PLAZAS, OPEN SPACE

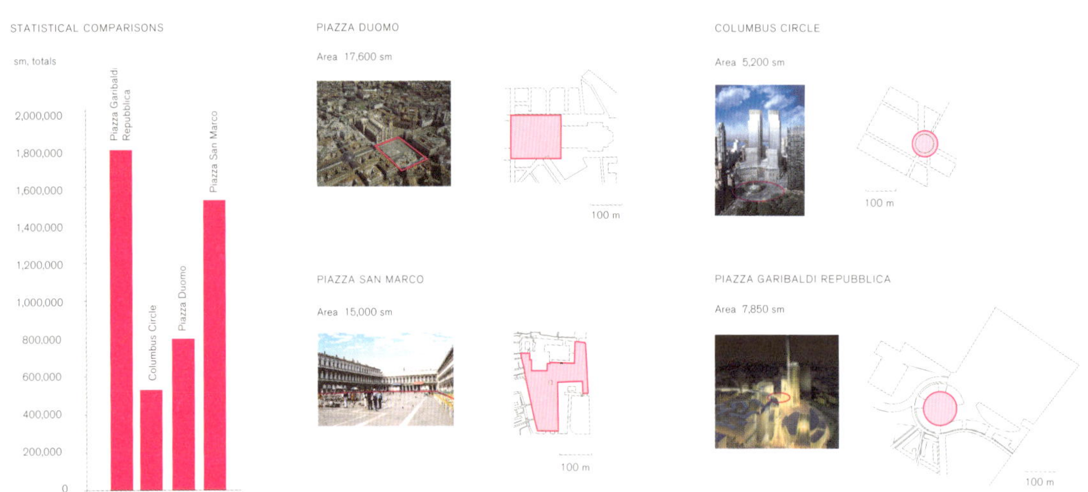

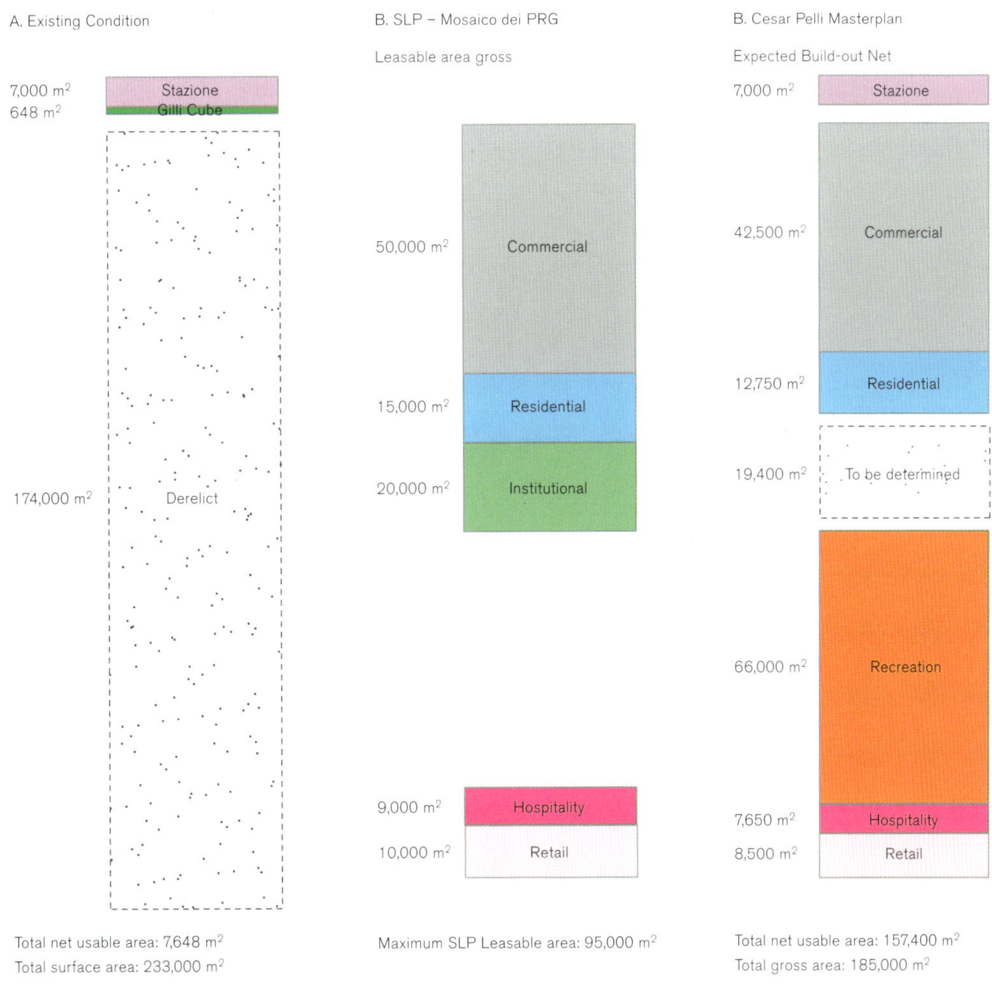

opposite: Scalar analysis of the Pelli Master Plan with other mixed-use urban redevelopments and public open spaces.

above: Comparison of the existing uses at Garibaldi Repubblica with the maximum allowable commercial floor area (SLP) and the total programmed area, private and public, in the Pelli Master Plan.

site plan 1:500

The revised plan for MOdAM by student Garo Balmanoukian consists of five courtyard blocks derived from a formal study of local building typologies in central Milan. The site plan is open-ended and flexible. It can grow and shift to accommodate changing exhibitions or additions to the building program. Pedestrian access to the park is channeled in between the five blocks, with porous façades allowing glimpses of the exhibitions and activities inside.

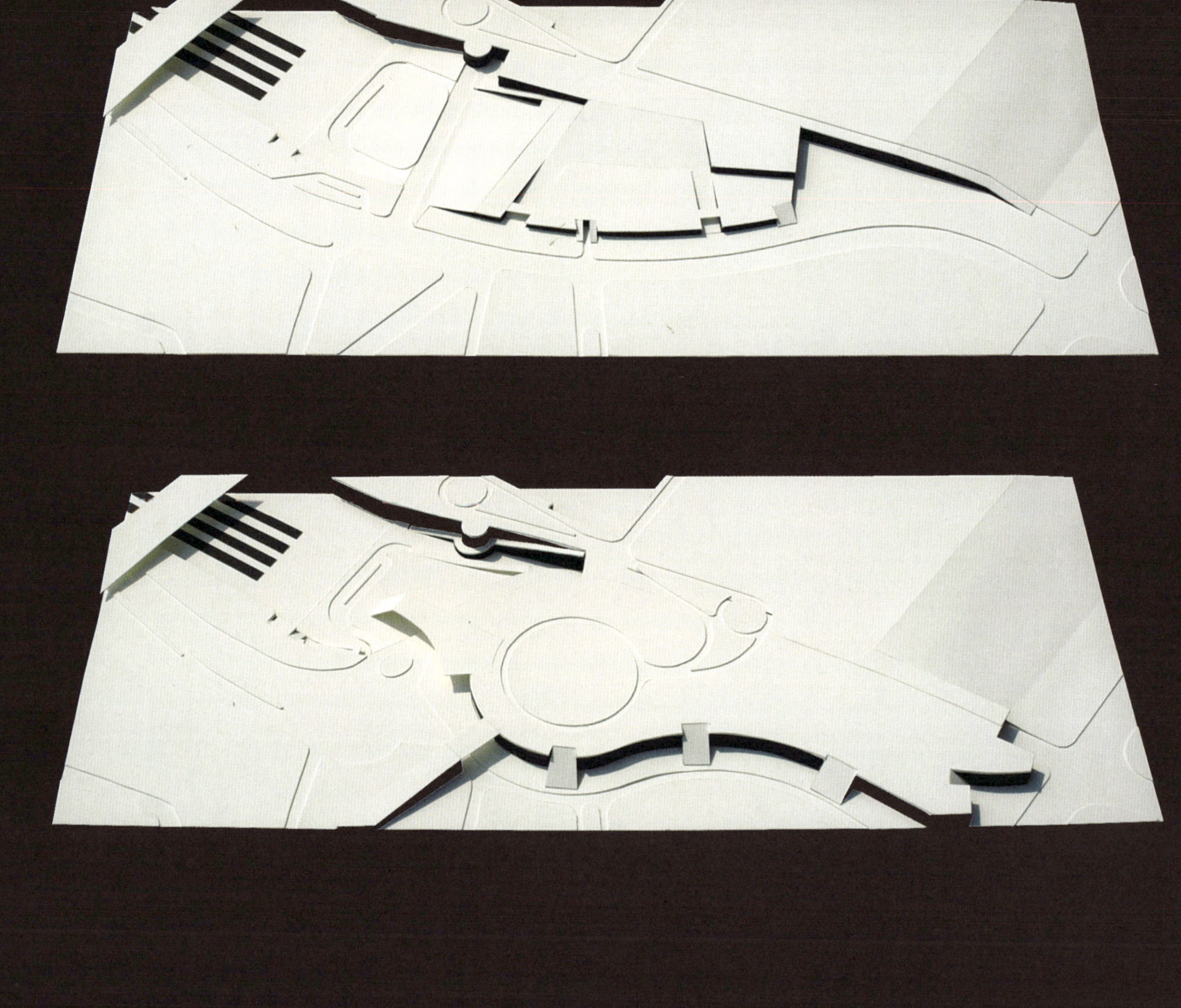

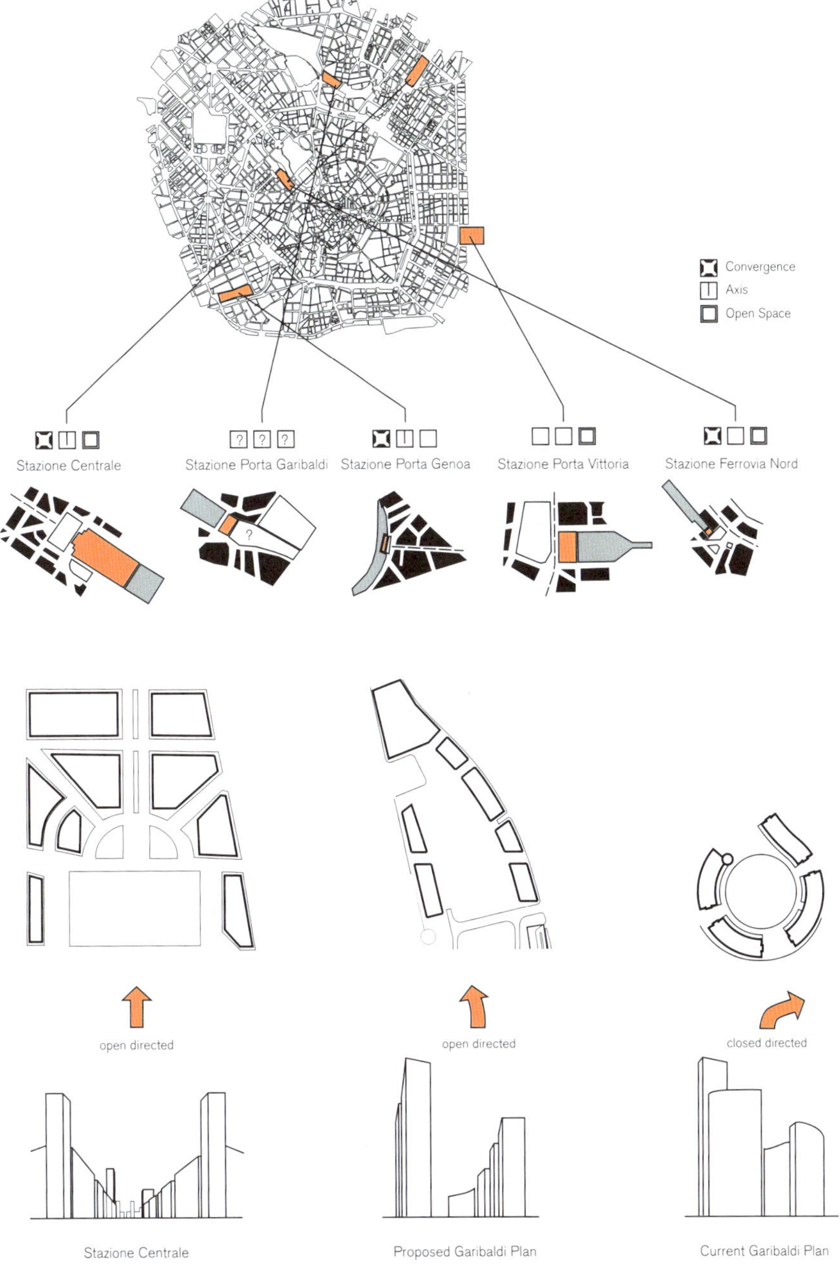

opposite: Two sketch models by Genevieve Fu and Brett Spearman reveal the urban implications of the current master plan. To accommodate parking with underground transportation infrastructure the Pelli plan (bottom) is forced to elevate the project on a 12-meter plinth, effectively producing a wall to the existing neighborhood. The revised plan (top) shifts the bulk of the parking along the highway (relocated from its place in the Pelli plan), allowing the impenetrable black foam of the plinth to be broken down in scale and made more accessible to the immediate context.

above: Analysis of the urban context of train stations in Milan revealed that the station is typically at the end of a central axis or similar formal progression. The Pelli Master Plan deviates from this convention: Traffic circulates around, not toward, the building, and the office towers appear to turn their backs to the station. A proposed plan restores the axial convention so that buildings define a green, landscaped corridor with the station at the terminus.

PROGRAM ANALYSIS

Stazione
Commercial
Residential
Recreation
Hospitality
Retail

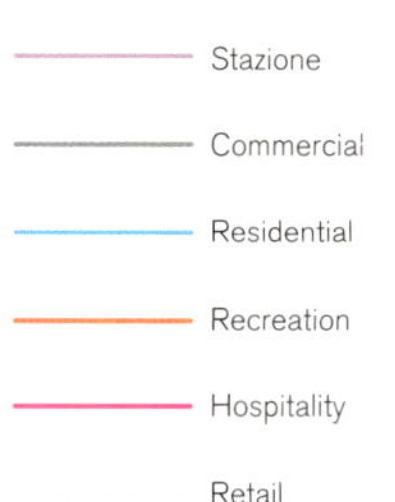

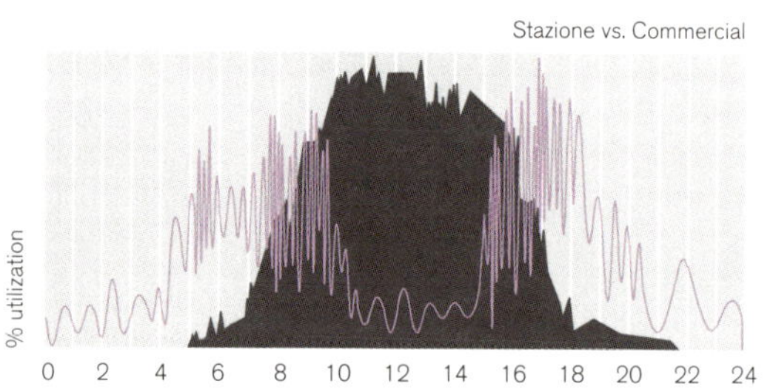

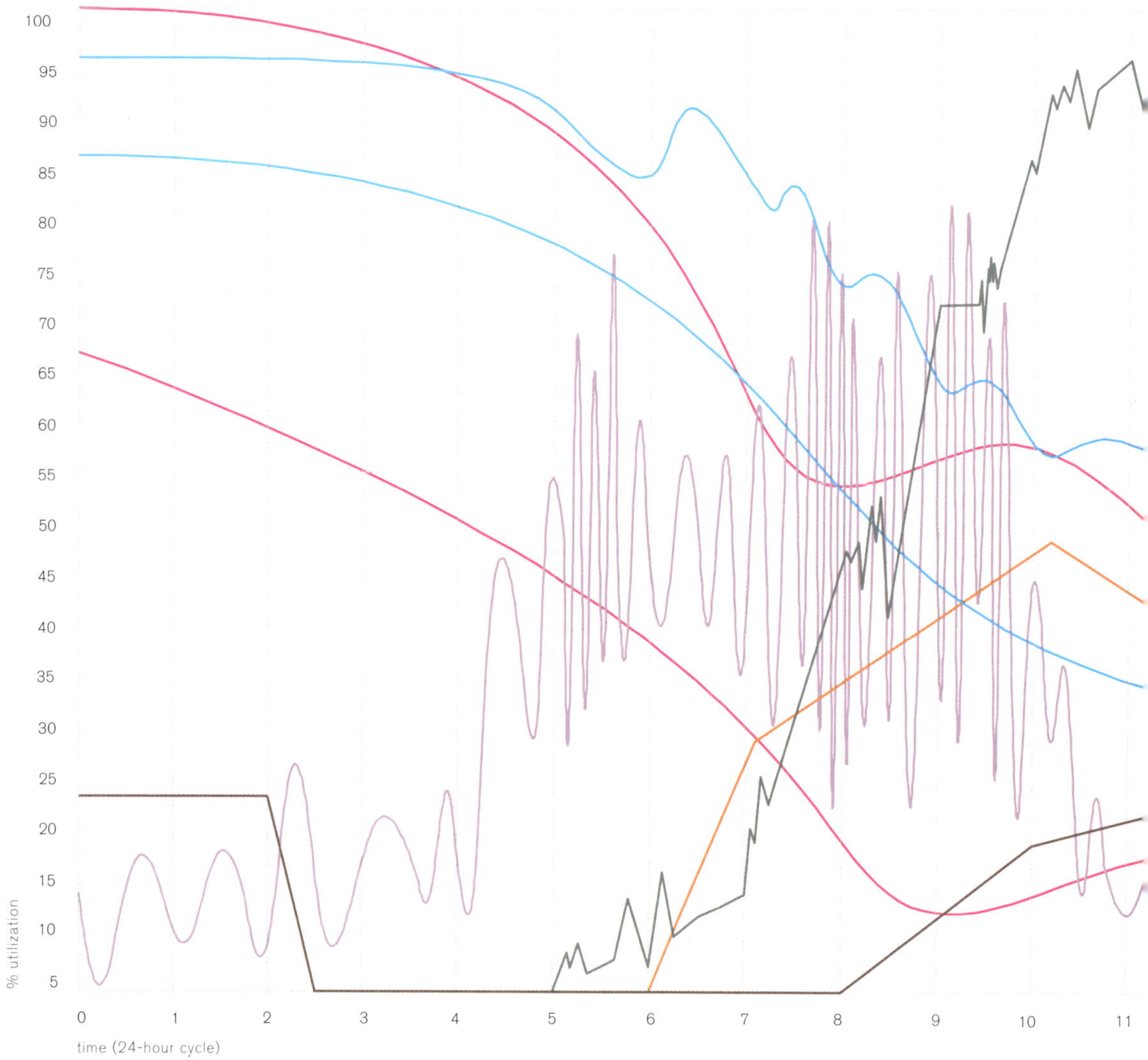

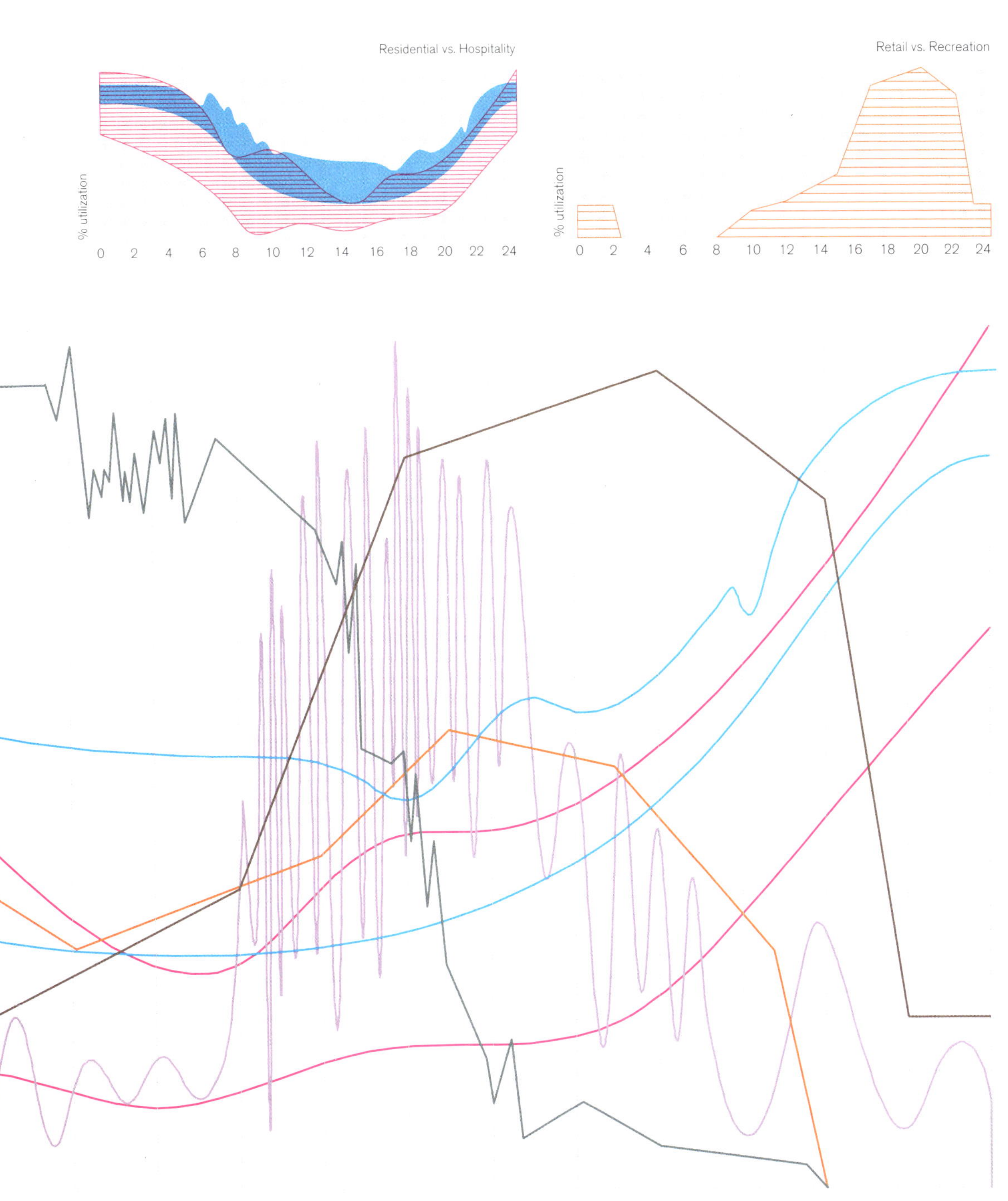

Graph of program for the Cesar Pelli Master Plan, showing changes in the intensity of use over a 24-hour cycle.

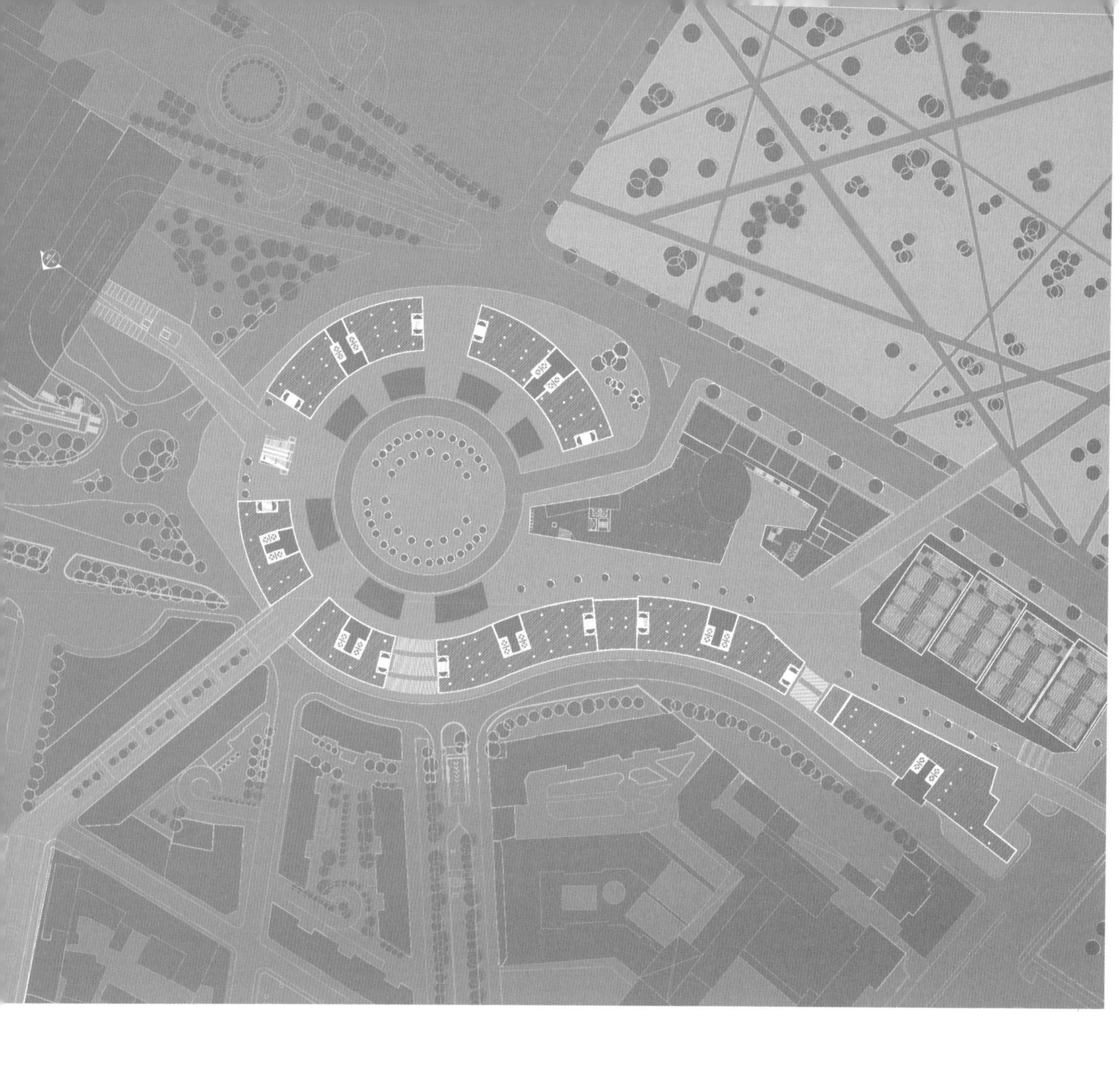

opposite: Three conclusions from an analysis of the Pelli proposal lead to a new master plan: 1) For the Hines project to be successful, it must generate a critical density of activity on the plinth. 2) The oversize piazza Garibaldi at the heart of the project is the biggest threat to this density; MOdAM must face and activate the piazza. 3) The park is also not an asset to the project; remove the canopy over Via del Nord connecting the park with Garibaldi Repubblica, and let MOdAM, like a wedge, fill in the void and generate density.

above: In student Benjamin Albertson and Marissa Browns' project, the ground is not solid but a contoured skin that extends a parklike landscape across the full site. But as a skin, the ground is active on both sides: Underneath are exhibition halls, parking, and the MOdAM school. Above are reciprocal programs: retail, restaurants, and the MOdAM museum, which break through the ground-surface to emerge as independent buildings.

III. MODAM YALE: THE BEHNISCH-HINES STUD

AT. MODAM YALE: THE BEHNISCH-HONES STUD

Programming and Organizational Diagrams

Milan for the first time in decades is redefining its architectural landscape by redeveloping areas of the city that have historically lain dormant. Followed by the recently completed fairgrounds (*Fiera Milano*), Garibaldi Repubblica is one of the largest and most ambitious master-planned redevelopments in Italy. The draft program for the development was written by the department of urban planning in Milan and established a set of ground rules for programming and maximum allowed floor area. The city's goal for the project is to satisfy the demand for modern, high-tech office space in a new mixed-use *Citta della Moda* (Fashion City) that will include residential, retail, and a generous park, in addition to a major fashion exhibition center and a new institution dedicated to Italian fashion, MOdAM, housing a design museum and fashion school.

The Foundation of Fashion, led by Gabriele Albertini, mayor of Milan, and Beatrice Trussardi, CEO of Trussardi group, wrote the program for MOdAM conceptualizing the institution as an incubator for fashion and contemporary culture. The design exploration of MOdAM in the Yale studio was an opportunity to test the foundation's ideas for the institution against the city's aspirations for the larger Garibaldi Repubblica project. The challenge for the studio was to leverage the specificity of MOdAM to make the Citta della Moda into a new destination for fashion and culture in Italy and, conversely, to find a way for the magnitude of the full project to reinvent this institution. Students, in analyzing the hybrid nature of the connected programs, developed concepts of flow, orientation, and adjacencies of programming, which were based on a given of the surrounding infrastructure as well as the client's minimum program demands. Applying architectural tools for process diagrams—such as "weaving the city fabric," "jigsaw pieces," "liquid fluidity," "pixelation," "frequencies," and "hybrid horizontal"—the students completed analysis appears in the following pages.

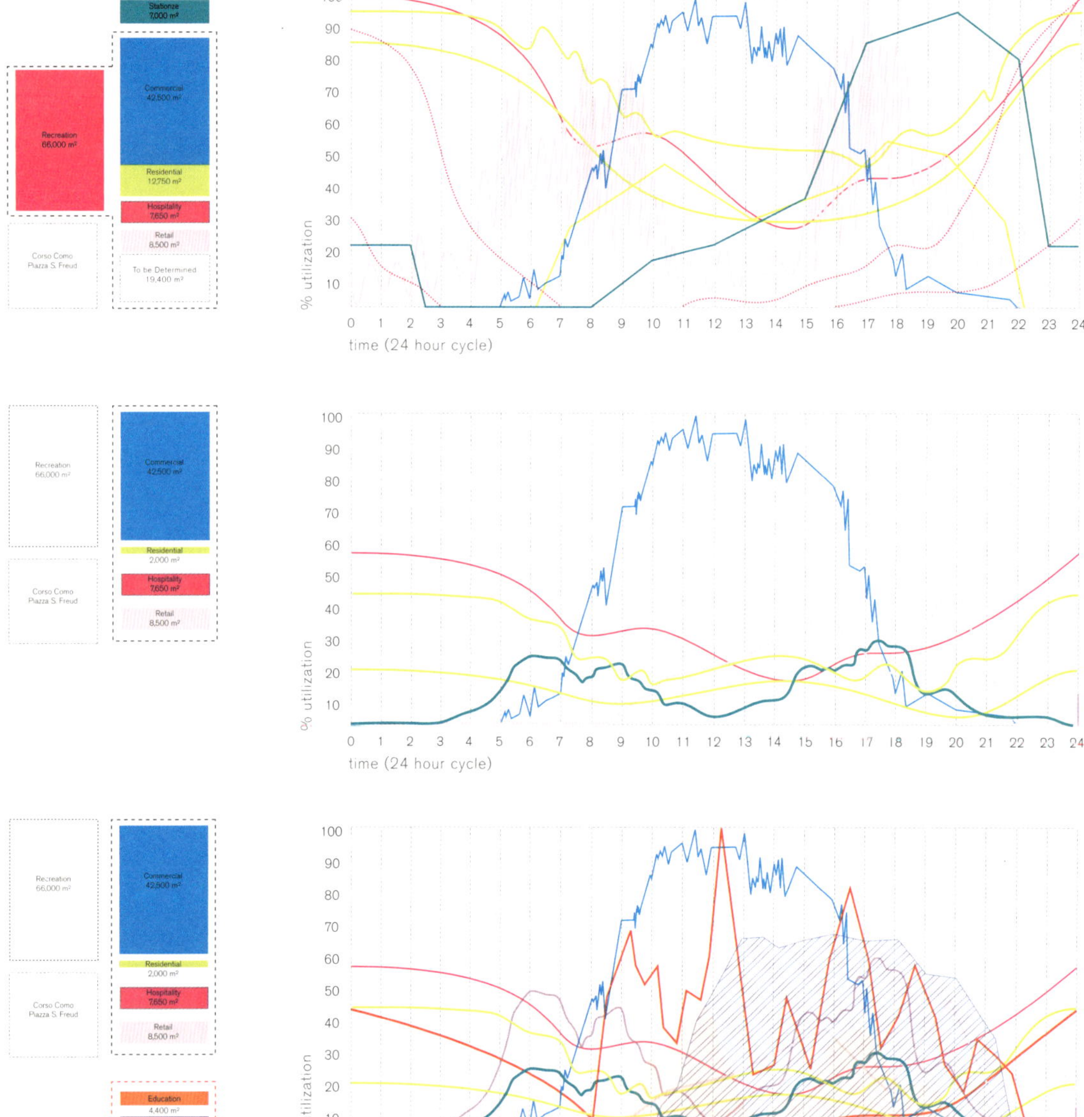
Stationze
7,000 m²
Recreation
66,000 m²
Commercial
42,500 m²
Residential
12,750 m²
Hospitality
7,650 m²
Retail
8,500 m²
Corso Como
Piazza S. Freud
To be Determined
19,400 m²
100
90
80
70
60
50
40
30
20
10
% utilization
0 1 2 3 4 5 6 7 8 9 10 11 12 13 14 15 16 17 18 19 20 21 22 23 24
time (24 hour cycle)
Recreation
66,000 m²
Commercial
42,500 m²
Residential
2,000 m²
Hospitality
7,650 m²
Retail
8,500 m²
Corso Como
Piazza S. Freud
100
90
80
70
60
50
40
30
20
10
% utilization
0 1 2 3 4 5 6 7 8 9 10 11 12 13 14 15 16 17 18 19 20 21 22 23 24
time (24 hour cycle)
Recreation
66,000 m²
Commercial
42,500 m²
Residential
2,000 m²
Hospitality
7,650 m²
Retail
8,500 m²
Corso Como
Piazza S. Freud
Education
4,400 m²
Institutional
4,000 m²
Exposition
10,000 m²
100
90
80
70
60
50
40
30
20
10
% utilization
0 1 2 3 4 5 6 7 8 9 10 11 12 13 14 15 16 17 18 19 20 21 22 23 24
time (24 hour cycle)

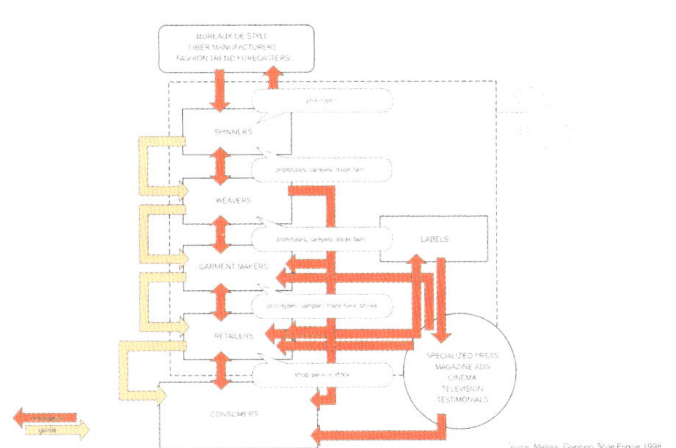

ITALIAN FASHION INDUSTRY

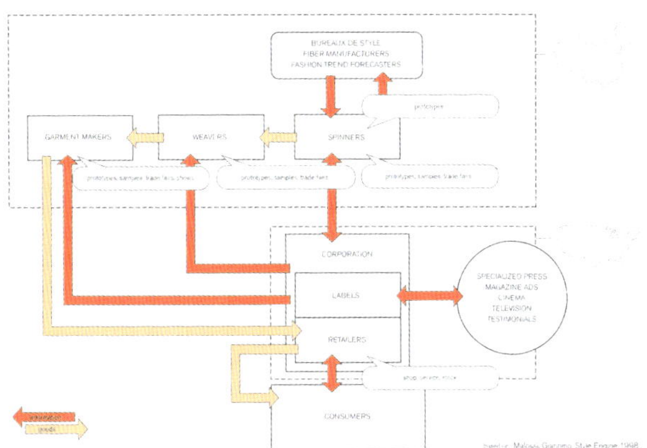

GLOBAL FASHION INDUSTRY

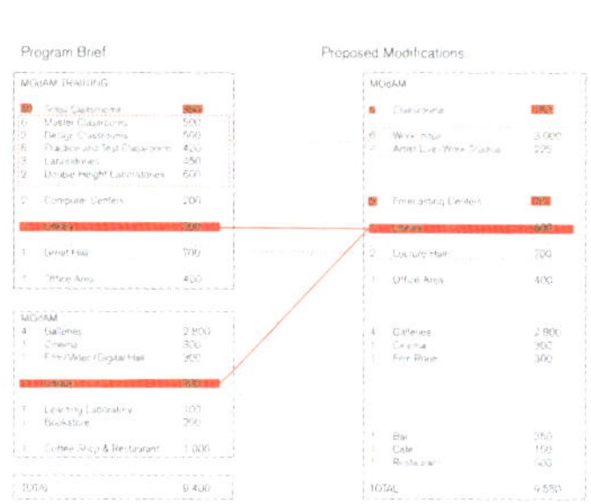

PROGRAM COMPARISON

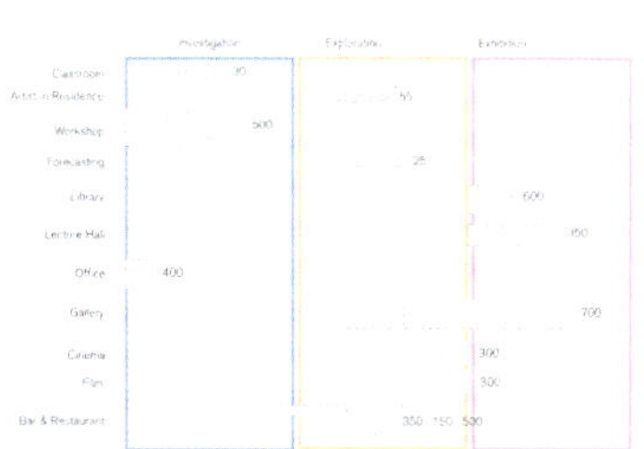

PROGRAMMATIC ZONES

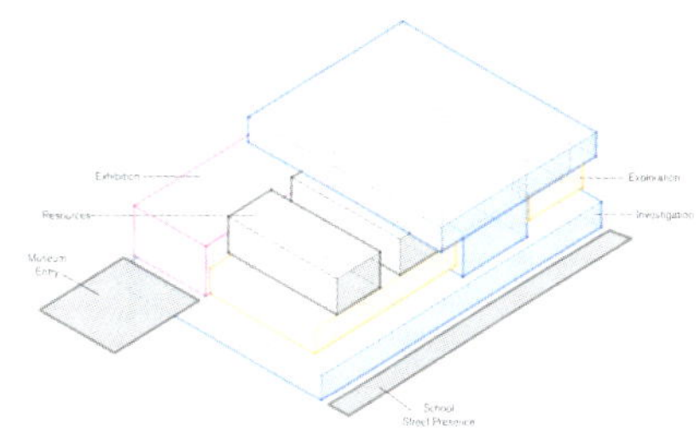

SECTIONAL ZONE ARRANGEMENT

opposite: For both the developer and the architect, the ultimate success of a large mixed-use project rests on its ability to integrate with its immediate context as an intensively utilized, 24-hour community. Analysis of the theoretical utilization of the Pelli Master Plan by program indicates a model mixed-use development (top image) that is active throughout the day. However, if this analysis concentrates on the plinth only (middle image), which contains the majority of the floor area of the project, a different picture emerges: heavy use during business hours, nearly no use in the evenings, mornings, or weekends. MOdAM has the capacity to change this by introducing a program that will have peak activity outside of standard working hours (bottom image). The mission of MOdAM is clear: save the plinth through a density of activity and occupation. Only then is there a chance to give the project the quality of life necessary to make it a new district for Milan.

above: The fashion industry in Italy is changing. Historically, its strength came from the integration of design and production. This is what the MADE IN ITALY label represents. Today, the fashion houses are still strong but the manufacturing component is facing stiff competition, mostly from Asian textile plants that are increasingly able to produce high-quality fabric and finished garments at a reduced cost. Within Italy, there is much resistance to the globalization of the fashion industry. The initiative to create MOdAM in Milan is one example. Architecture can also play a role. The programmatic organization of MOdAM replicates the traditional vertical integration of design and production by clustering the museum and school around a "cross-pollination area," bringing together designers and business students at MOdAM with small workshops in a central zone that draws on the resources of the entire building.

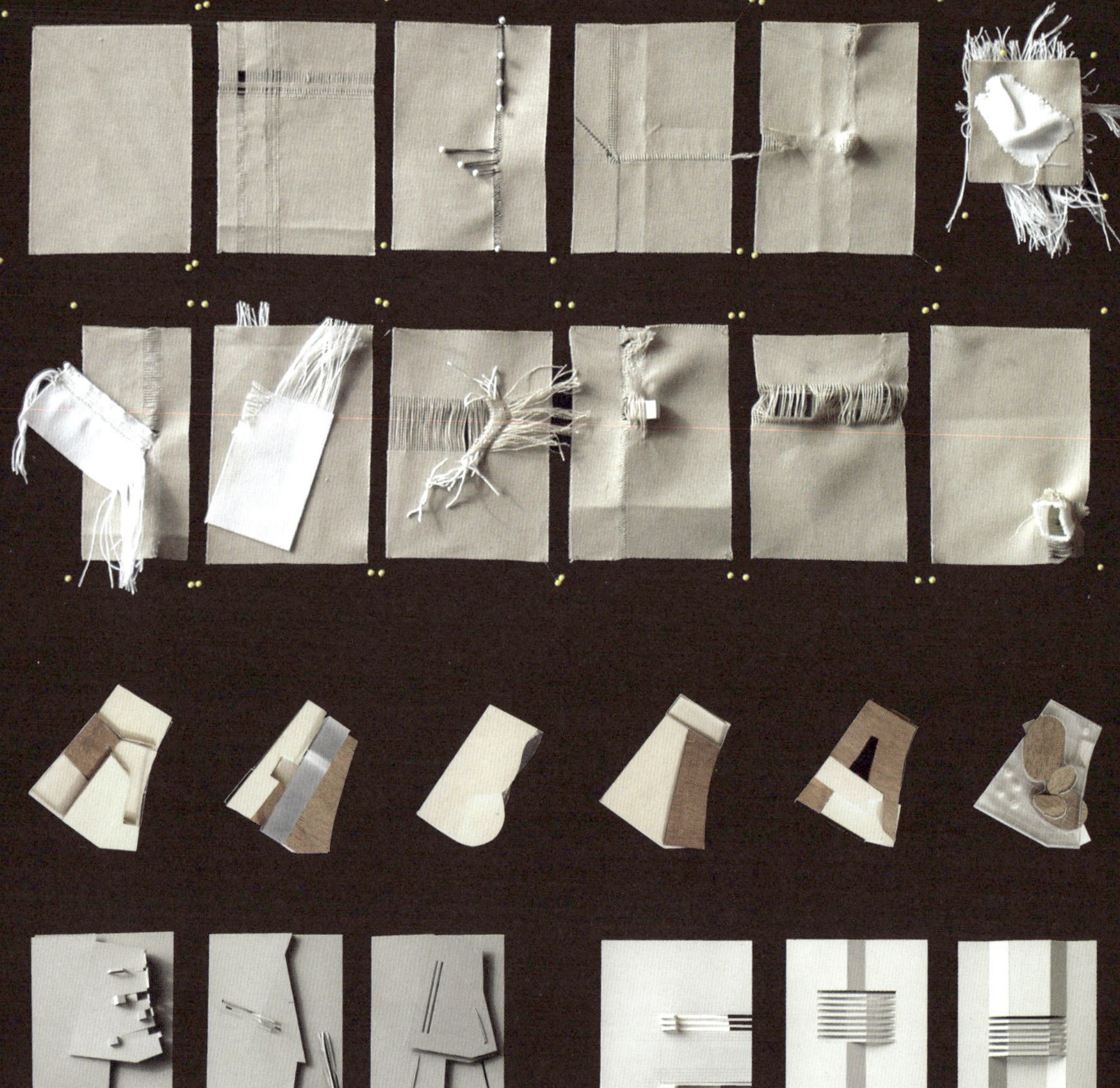

above and opposite: Weaving strives for regularity. The strength of fabric comes from the repetition of a single pattern. However, in this uniformity there is also the potential for distortion using many of the same techniques that otherwise yield a regular weave. The metaphor of weaving can be applied to buildings, and, likewise, the potential for distortion of the weave can be translated into an architectonic condition.

Experimentation with fabric produced a set of techniques for use in the design of MOdAM by students Genevieve Fu and Brett Spearman: above, from top: *extraction*, the removal of thread; *dislocation*, where tension on one part of the cloth produces irregularities in other parts; *merging*, when two fabrics are woven together, their organizations overlap; *pivot*, the introduction of a tool; *pimple*, the introduction of a foreign object.

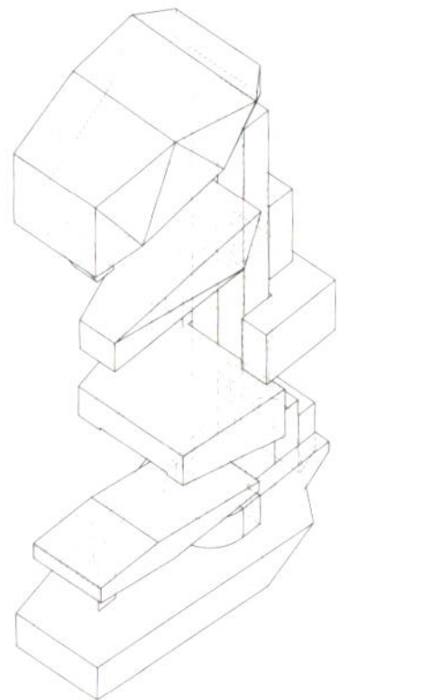
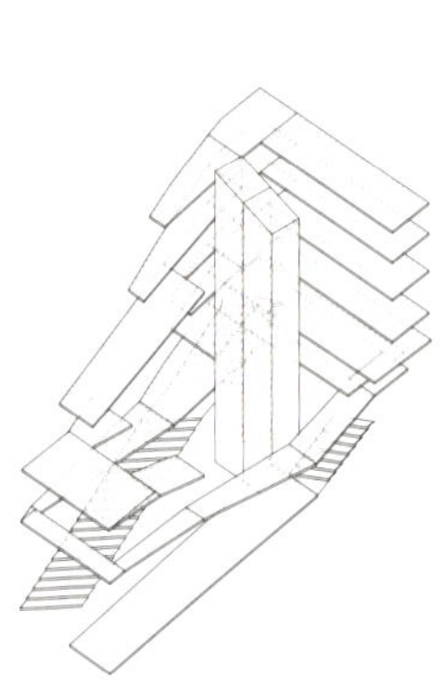
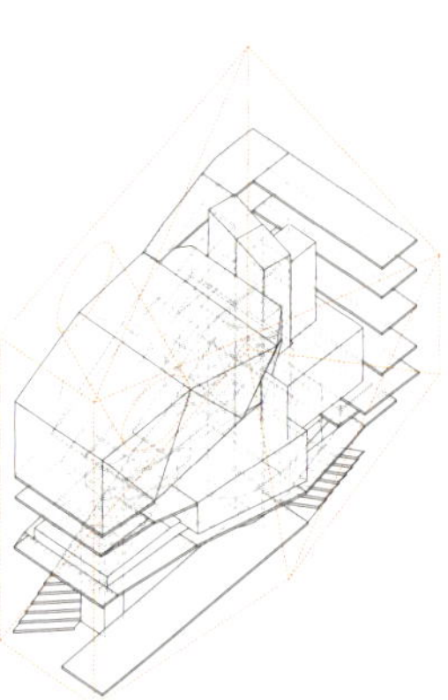
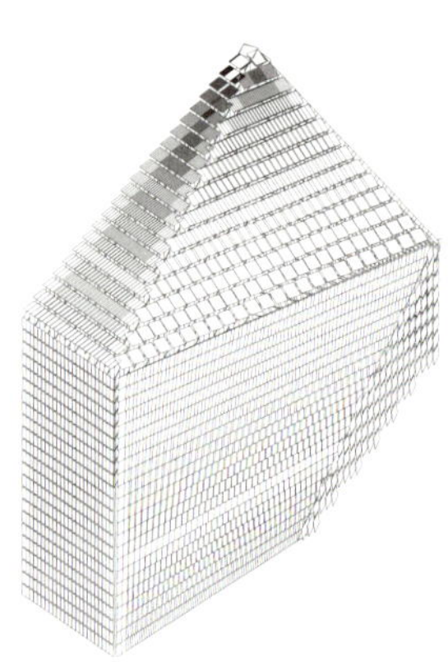

MOdAM Museum

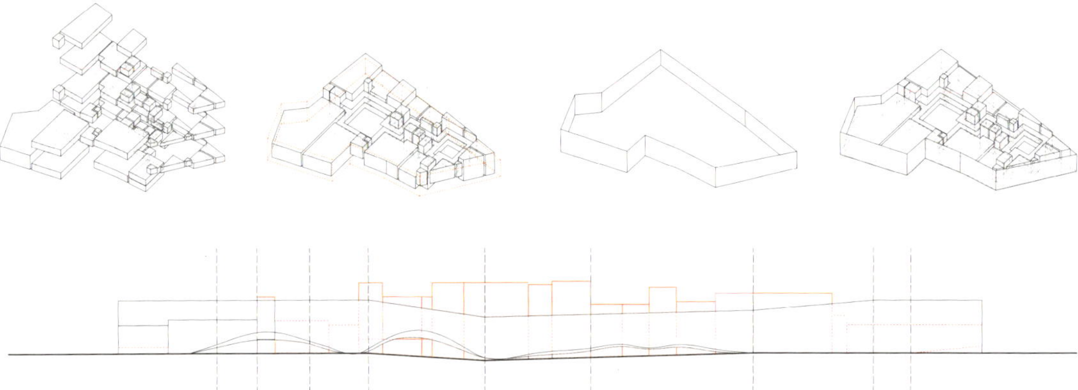

MOdAM School

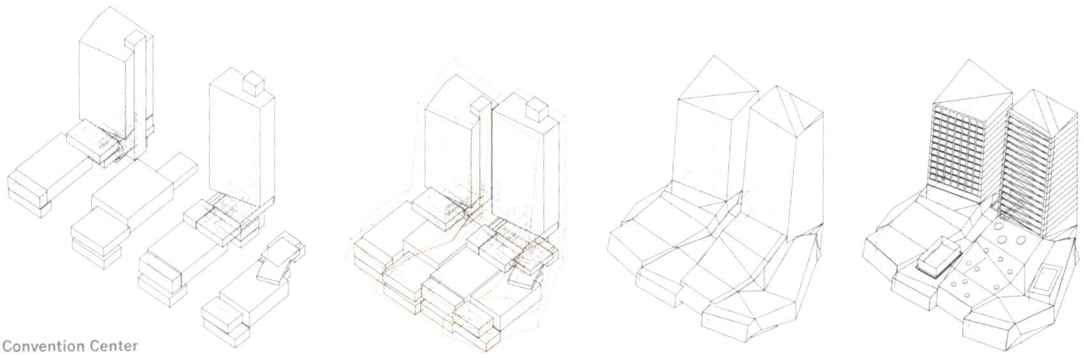

Convention Center

above and opposite: Three buildings are elaborated in three diagrams by students Forth Bagley and Jonah Gamblin. First, the museum (top row): elements with a fixed program—cinema, library, etc.—are stacked with a vertical circulation core. Between these elements and the building enclosure is a continuous, unfixed residual zone, sometime gallery, sometime gift store but always flexible. Second, the school (middle row): similar program elements stack vertically, (a small classroom tower, a small lecture-hall tower). A continuous wall wraps these towers. The wall is like a set piece, shaped by its context: On one side, it pulls in to define a piazza; on another, it pushes out to define a street edge. Finally, the convention center (bottom row): four exhibition halls in a row, with a residential tower landing on the first and a hotel on the third. A surface drapes the unwieldy conglomeration.

RESTAURANT
GALLERY 4
GALLERY 5
GALLERY 1
BOOKSTORE
GREAT HALL
MODAM
LOBBY
TEMPORARY EXHIBITION
DIGITAL VIDEO AND FILM
TEMPORARY EXHIBITION
INTERNET AREA
PROJECT ROOMS
PROJECT ROOMS
LECTURE HALL
LECTURE HALL
LECTURE HALL

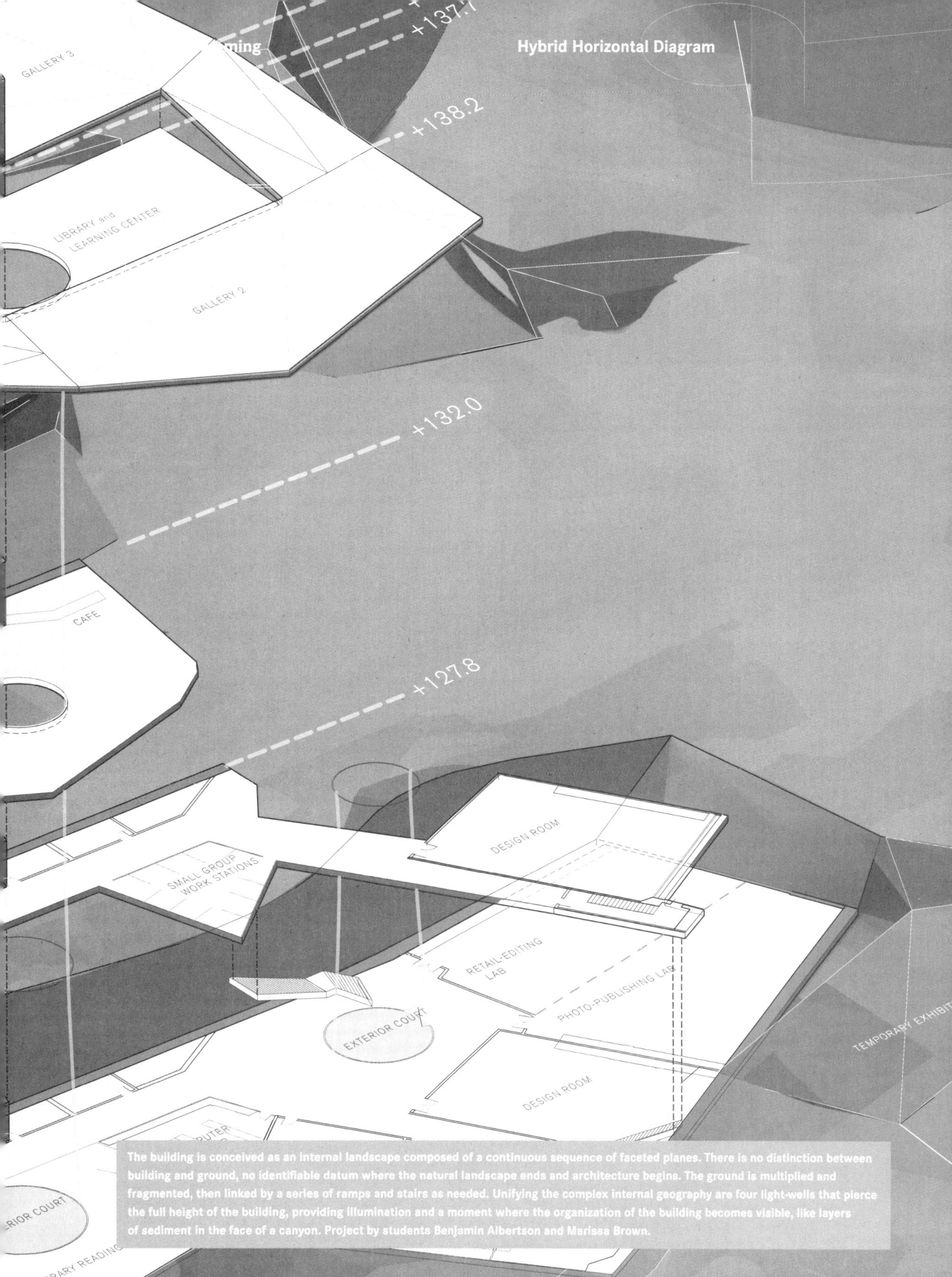

The building is conceived as an internal landscape composed of a continuous sequence of faceted planes. There is no distinction between building and ground, no identifiable datum where the natural landscape ends and architecture begins. The ground is multiplied and fragmented, then linked by a series of ramps and stairs as needed. Unifying the complex internal geography are four light-wells that pierce the full height of the building, providing illumination and a moment where the organization of the building becomes visible, like layers of sediment in the face of a canyon. Project by students Benjamin Albertson and Marissa Brown.

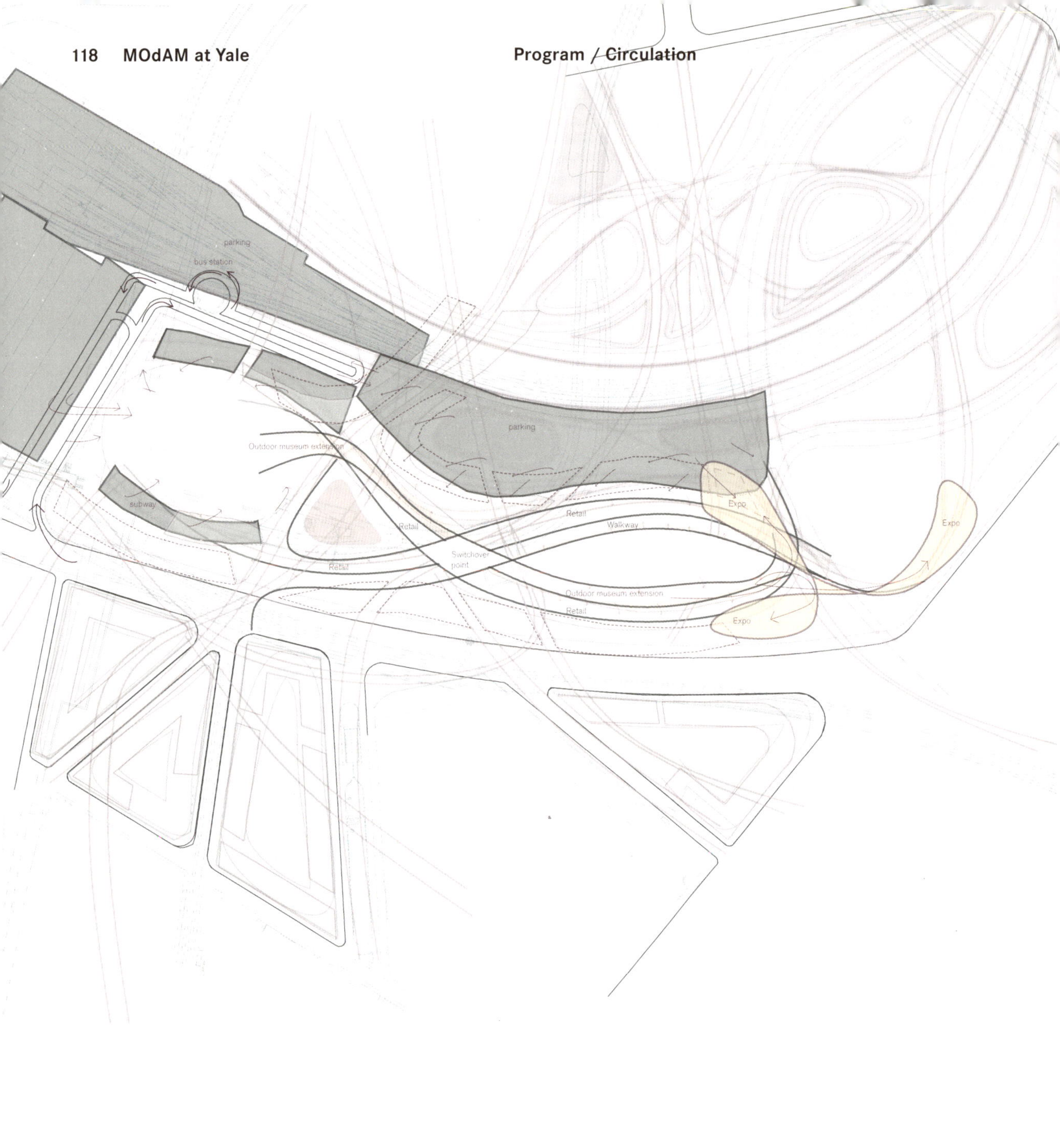
parking
bus station
parking
Outdoor museum extension
subway
Retail
Retail
Walkway
Switchover point
Retail
Outdoor museum extension
Retail
Expo
Expo
Expo

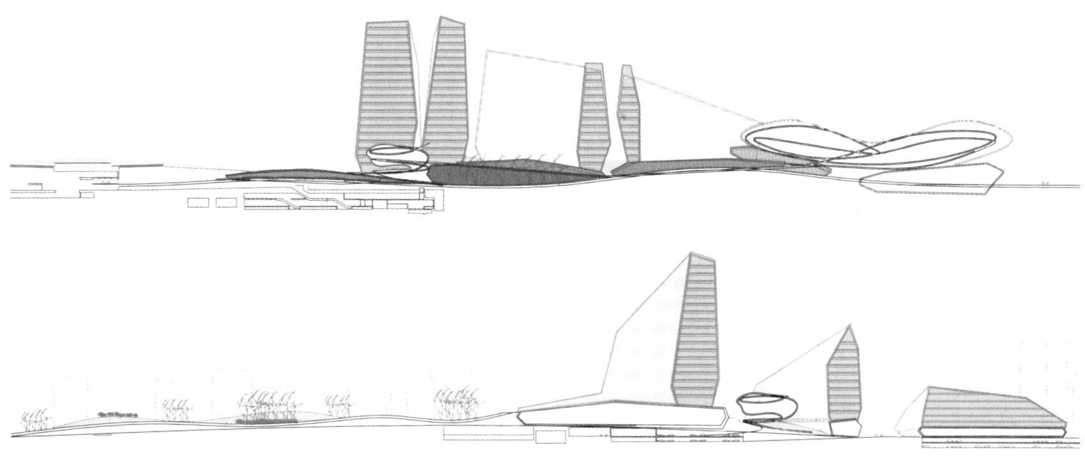

opposite and above: Circulation is first, the architecture follows. The urban and architectural diagrams of the project by students Ceren Bingol and Jennifer Newsom are developed from studying the circulation flows on the site and in the building. Underlying the master plan is a series of circuits, closed loops that wrap the site. The building for MOdAM is a three-legged loop that enables three distinct user-groups—museum visitors, students, and passersby—to traverse the entire building independently without a dead end or a restricted entry. Externally, the three loops of MOdAM form a three-way arch that is positioned as a gateway to the Garibaldi Repubblica project at the nexus of vehicular traffic. Here, all the loops collide: infrastructure, urban, and architectural.

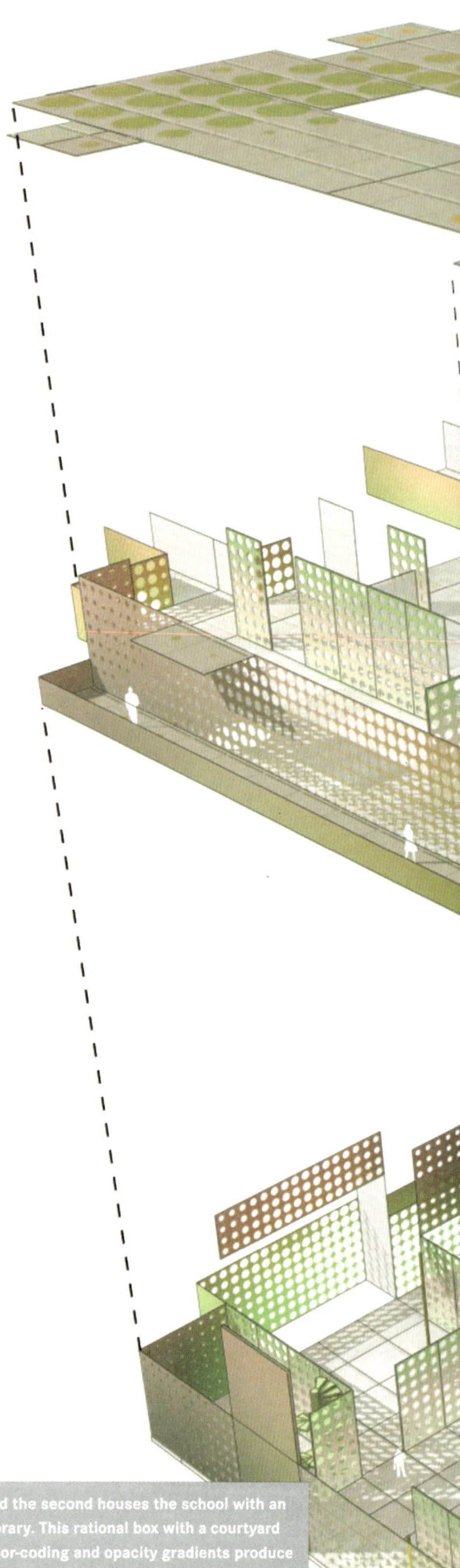

The first floor of the building in the student project by Garo Balmanoukian houses the museum, and the second houses the school with an overlap zone between the two for shared resources, such as a computing center, a theater, and a library. This rational box with a courtyard is animated by a façade system that corresponds to the internal program areas of the building. Color-coding and opacity gradients produce a pixilated enclosure that reveals or conceals the activities as needed.

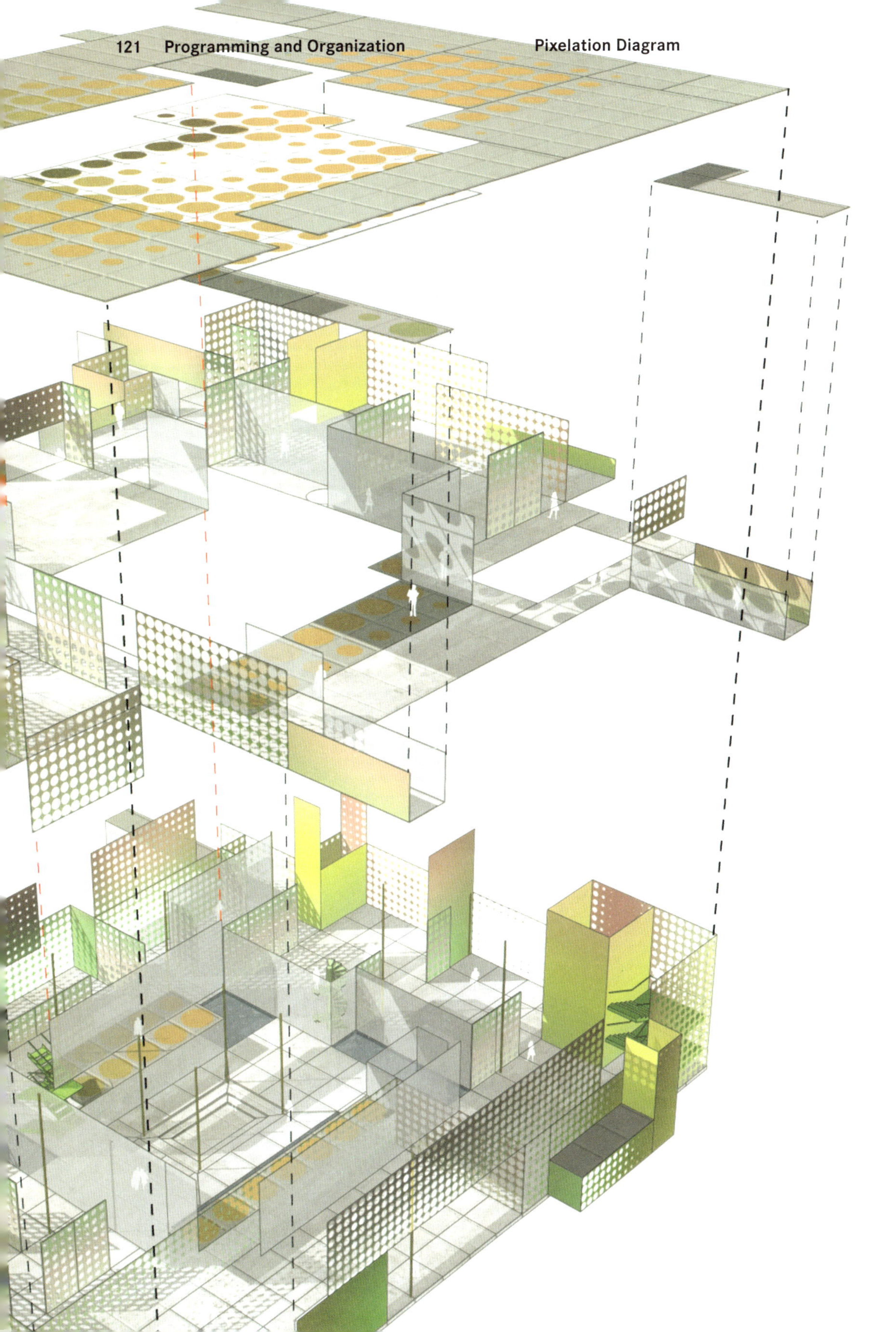

Public Space

The Pelli Master Plan for Garibaldi Repubblica designates a strip of land for MOdAM that is poised between the Hines' commercial development on one side and a new public park by Michael Maltzan and Petra Blaisse with their team INSIDE/OUTSIDE on the other. Motivated by city politics and entitlement risks rather than urban design strategy, the proposed site is neither part of the landscape nor the city. The design of MOdAM and its public spaces requires reconciliation on the part of the architect between the open space of the park and the dense social character of the piazza as both a solution to the indecisive master plan and a model for MOdAM within the public spaces of Garibaldi Repubblica. The student explorations of public space found meaning in its value as a draw for economic and civic vitality.

Two competing student models for public open space emerged in the studio: "the park" and "the piazza." Proponents of the park model emphasized continuity between architecture and landscape and used the design of MOdAM as a basis for site and landscape strategies that focused more on modulation and connection than edges and boundaries, creating projects such as "landscape piazza as park." Those working with the piazza model minimized the landscape component and instead used architecture to define a dense and intensively utilized urban condition in the public spaces of the project, resulting in projects such as "fluid piazza."

Piazzas

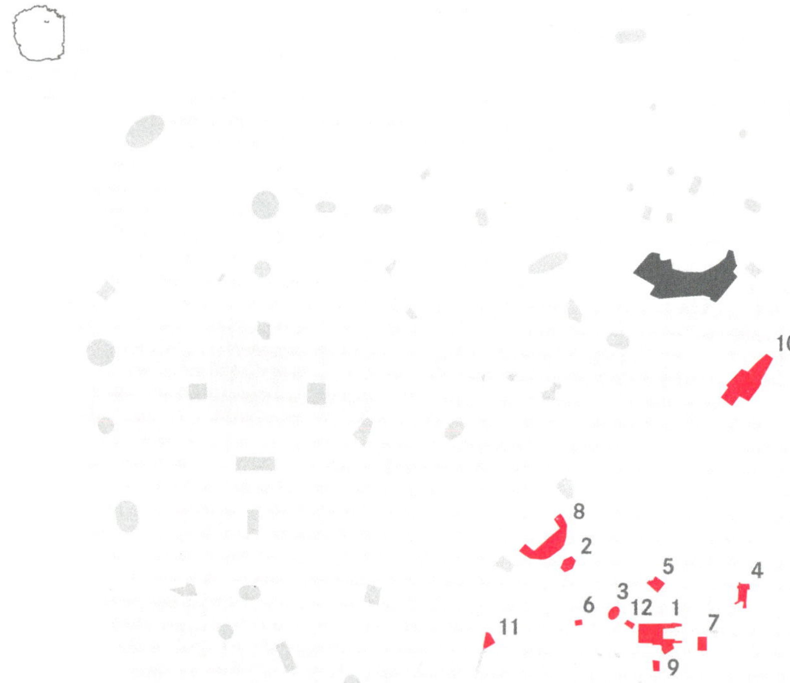

GARIBALDI REPUBBLICA (proposed)

1 PIAZZA DEL DUOMO

2 PIAZZA CAIROLI

3 PIAZZA CORDUSIO

4 PIAZZA SAN BABILA

5 PIAZZA DELLA SCALA

6 PIAZZA DEGLI AFFARI

7 PIAZZA FONTANA

8 PIAZZA CASTELLO

9 PIAZZA DIAZ

10 PIAZZA DELLA REPUBBLICA

11 PIAZZA SANT'AMBROGIO

12 PIAZZA MERCANTI

Parks

GARIBALDI REPUBBLICA (proposed)

1 PARCO SEMPIONE

2 GIARDINI PUBBLICI

3 GIARDINI DI VILLA REALE

4 ORTO BOTANICO

5 GIARDINO GUASTALLA

6 PARCO SOLARI

7 PARCO DELLE BASILICHE / PIAZZA DELLA VETRA

8 PARCO RAVIZZA

9 PARCO FORMENTANO / MARINAI D'ITALIA

10.46% of urban area is green-space use. 3,500 acres are publicly accessible.

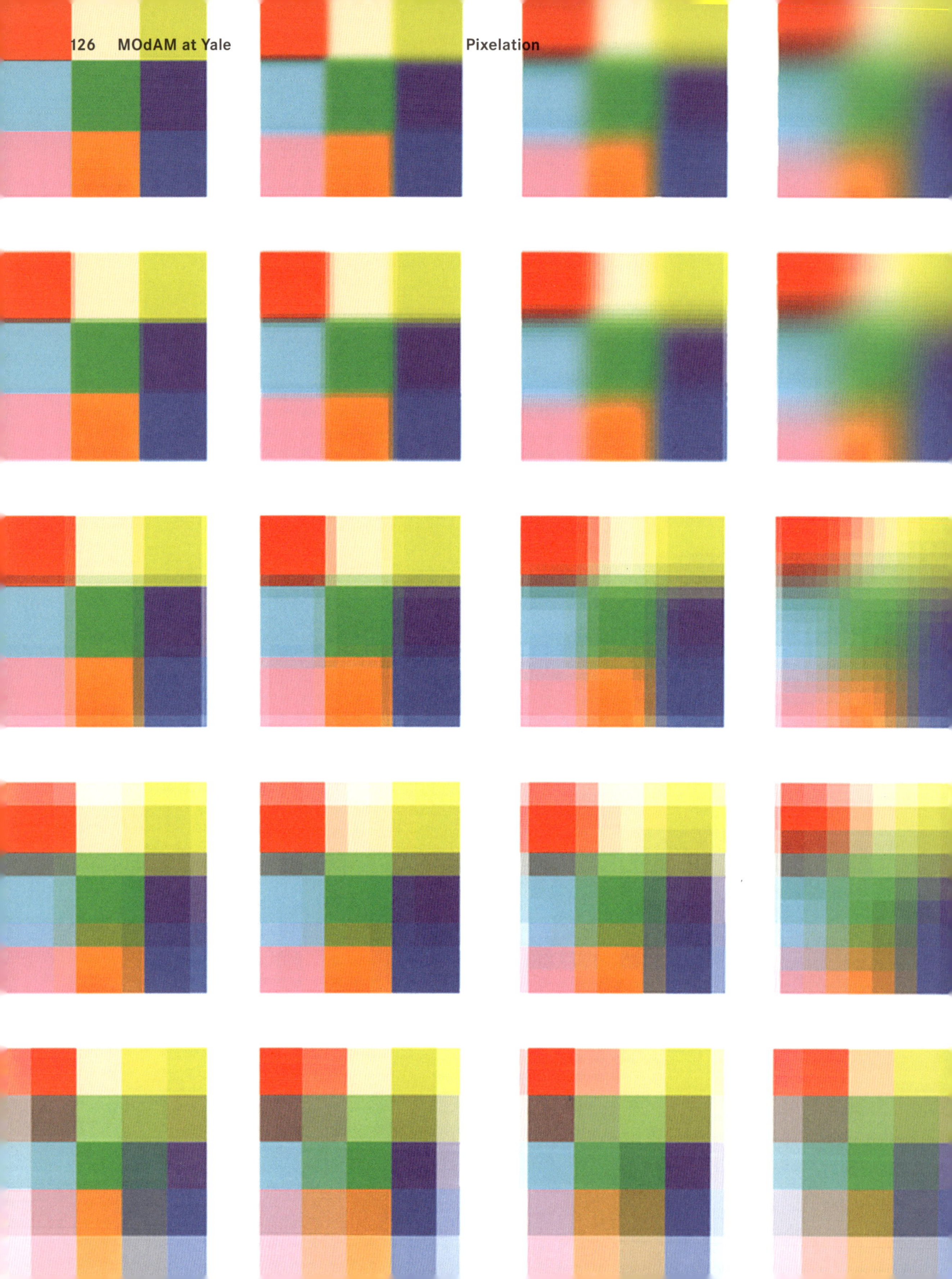

Milan Elevation Study

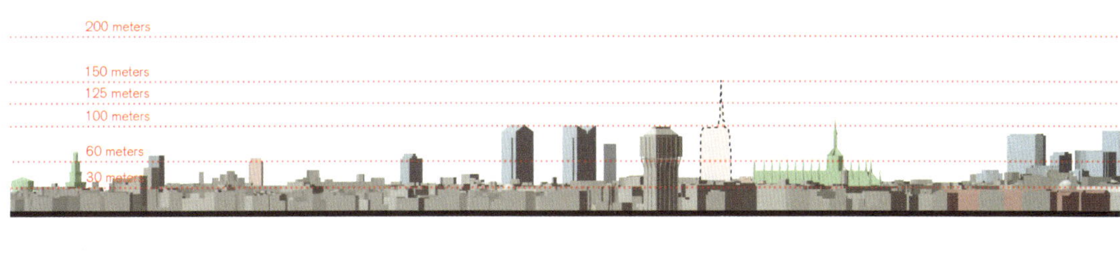

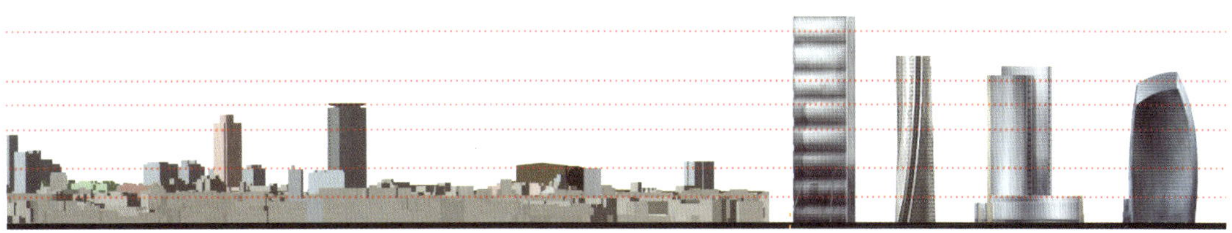

opposite: An initial study by student Garo Balmanoukian of pixilation as an open-space design strategy. Gaussian blurs were applied to a grid of color to simulate the overlap of programmed areas in landscape. The blur is multiplied from nine colors to many. A grid can then be reapplied to the blur to return to a discrete set of colors, but instead of the original pure colors, there are now nine hybrids.

above: The skyline of Milan with the proposed developments at Garibaldi Repubblica and the old Fiera. Rarely have buildings in Milan ever ascended past the spires of the Duomo.

Result of a formal analysis by student Garo Balmanoukian of buildings in central Milan that considered typical block sizes, gross cubic area, building types, and planning methodologies. Key to understanding the urban patterns in Milan is the relationships of scale from building to building and from building to open space. This diagram exaggerates these ratios to show areas of conformity and instances of variation.

As discussed at the studio review for students Benjamin Albertson and Marissa Brown:

Robert Stern: Is there a series of places where the building erupts out in relation to the exhibition hall?

Rafael Viñoly: It is a completely different question for me. It is a question of critical mass for the topographical idea to verify. If you have three times this material, then it's more of a systemic thing. If you have just this, it's a building. And your building is underground, partially.

Mark Simon: It is a little like the sea-monster sculpture, where you see the head of the sea monster coming out of the park or out of the sea, and then you see another piece.

Rafael Viñoly: It is a great moment for the public to see the connection.

opposite and above: Sketch renderings of the organizational relationship between MOdAM and the topographic surface that contains exhibition halls and other leisure programs. By Benjamin Albertson and Marissa Brown.

Real estate typically does not succeed in isolation; location is a primary driver of a property's market value. Yet for all its power, the influence of location is notoriously fickle and nearly impossible to define. More often than not, for a location to have a positive impact on real estate, it must first have a critical mass. Offices in central business districts lease better than those on the periphery simply because occupiers perceive a value in being near their competitors, as if the presence of one validates the others. For retail, location is an even greater factor, because retail tenants are highly dependent on access to the appropriate customer base. As an entirely new district of Milan, location is of fundamental concern for Garibaldi Repubblica. As in student Ceren Bingol's project, the development must invent its location and internally generate its own critical mass. Only then could the project capitalize on the full potential value of its real estate development.

Circulation and Infrastructure

It would be cliché but not untrue to say that the first question asked by the developers in the studio was: "Where is the front door?" And second: "Where can I park my car?" Their point was that for a public building like MOdAM, access is fundamental. But circulation is not only about access, it is also about experience. In the studio, the circulation design had to consider not only the connection to a very large and complex infrastructure at Garibaldi Repubblica, often noted as having the greatest concentration of transportation in northern Italy, but also the need to provide for all the close and discrete events—exhibition, education, culture, performance—that make up the MOdAM fashion museum and school.

For a public building, the internal circulation can be considered an extension of the general infrastructure network of the city. Circulation is the thread that ties the public program of the building to its city and its constituents. The design of the sequence of spaces that lead from the street into the institution is more than a solution to the problem of access or organization. Circulation is the means by which architecture can articulate and give meaning to the relationship between a public institution and the public that it serves. Each student project focused on various interpretations through design strategies such as plinth, public/private, horizontal flow, vertical flow, roofscape as runway, and unfolded space.

Rail / Tram / Bus

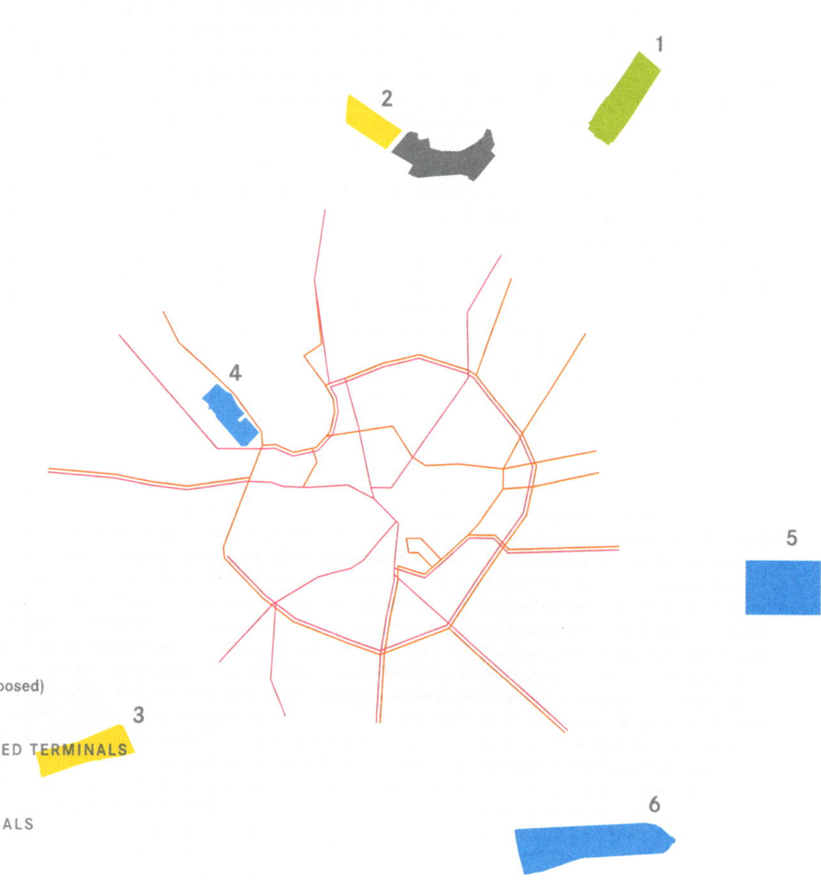

GARIBALDI REPUBBLICA (proposed)

INTERNATIONAL / HIGH SPEED TERMINALS

REGIONAL TERMINALS

LOCAL / SUBURBAN TERMINALS

TRAM ROUTE

BUS ROUTE

1 STAZIONE CENTRALE

2 STAZIONE PORTA GARIBALDI

3 STAZIONE PORTA GENOVA

4 STAZIONE FERROVIE NORD

5 STAZIONE PORTA VITTORIA

6 STAZIONE PORTA ROMANA

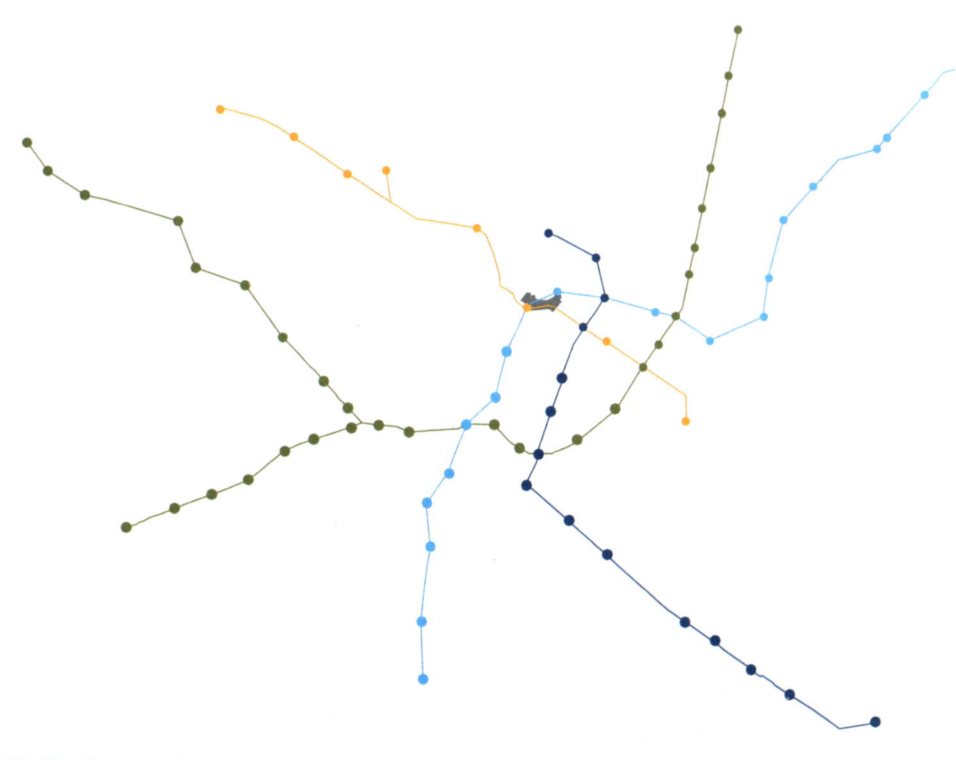

GARIBALDI REPUBBLICA (proposed)

MODE OF TRANSPORTATION (by frequency of use)

PUBLIC TRANSPORT / 42%

CAR / 43%

MOTORCYCLES / 4%

CAR PASSENGERS / 9%

OTHER / 3%

LINE M1

LINE M2

LINE M3

PASSANTE

A fifth line is planned and partially funded.

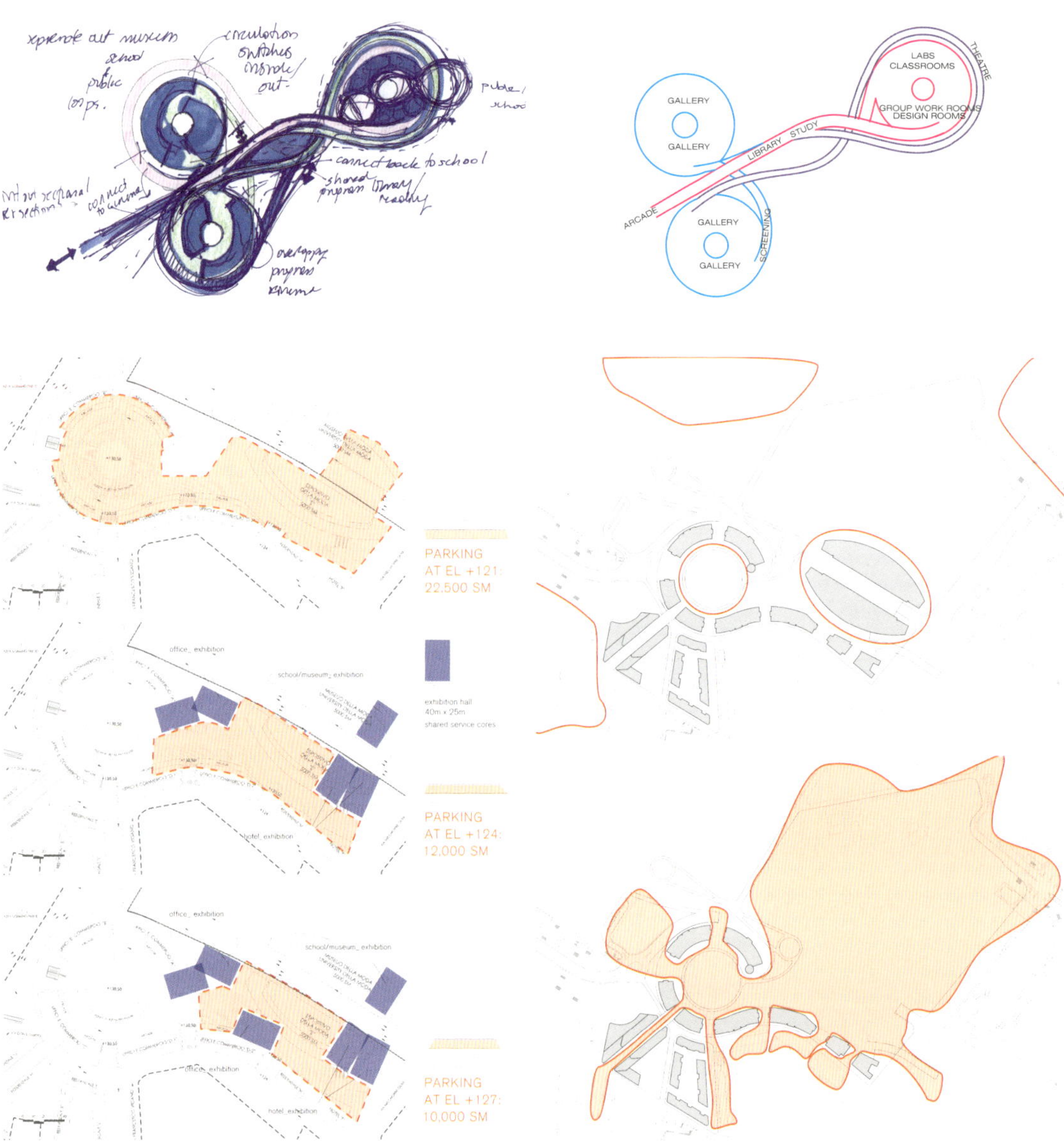

Circulation is not just a matter of where you can go but whether or not you would like to go there. What if the city was more like a park, as in the student project by Ceren Bingol (top)? What if the stroll through the piazza at Garibaldi Repubblica was more like the environment of an English garden than the football-field-size open space as proposed by Cesar Pelli, as in the student project by Benjamin Albertson and Marissa Brown (bottom and opposite)? How would this change use patterns? What line would one take from point A to point B? In Pelli's Master Plan, the movement is directed: One must circulate along the perimeter past the restaurants and boutiques on the ground floors of the buildings. In a park, movement is dispersed, more irregular, and the amenities locked-in the ground floors of the office towers in the Pelli plan are likewise liberally distributed across the site.

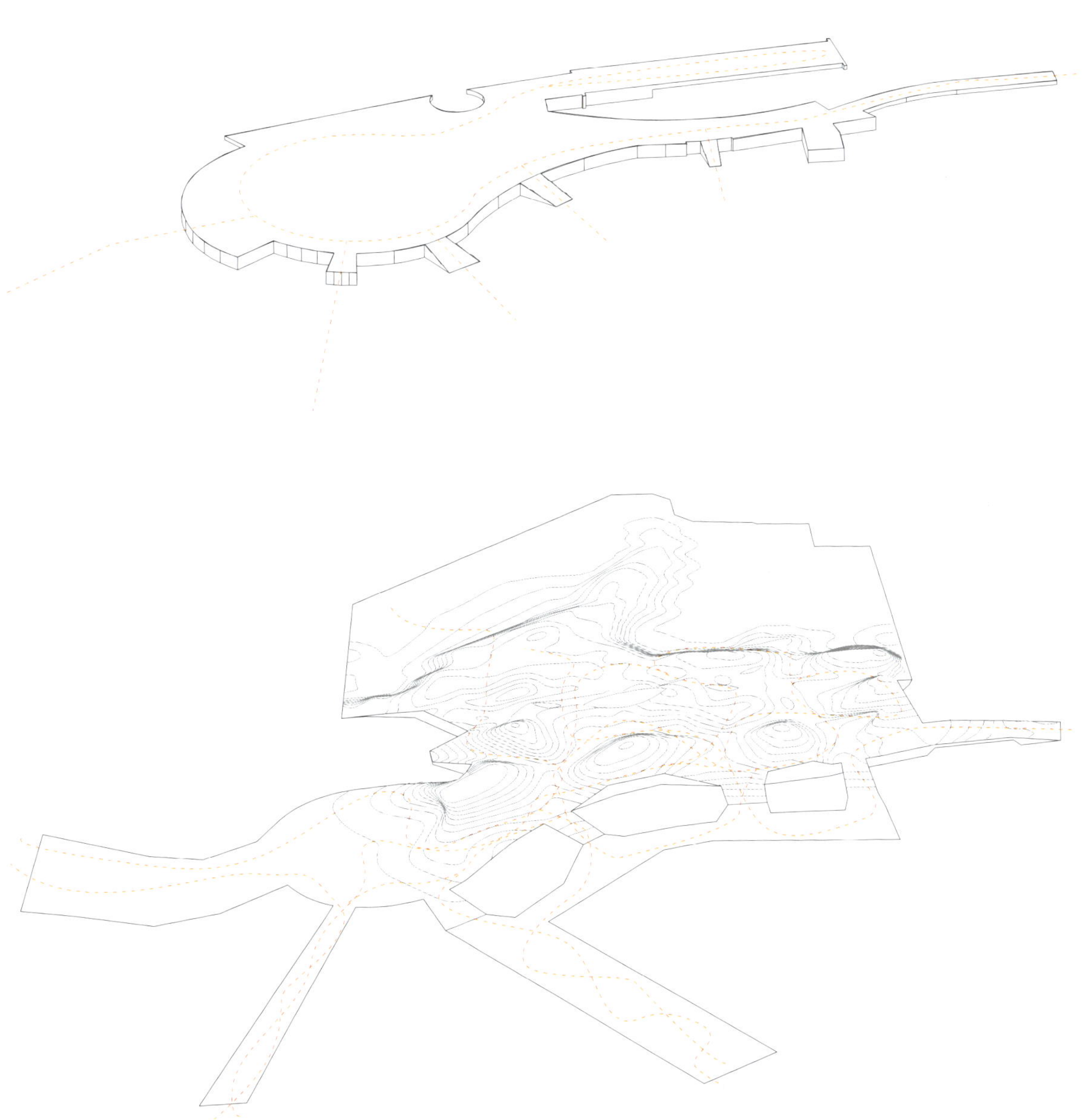

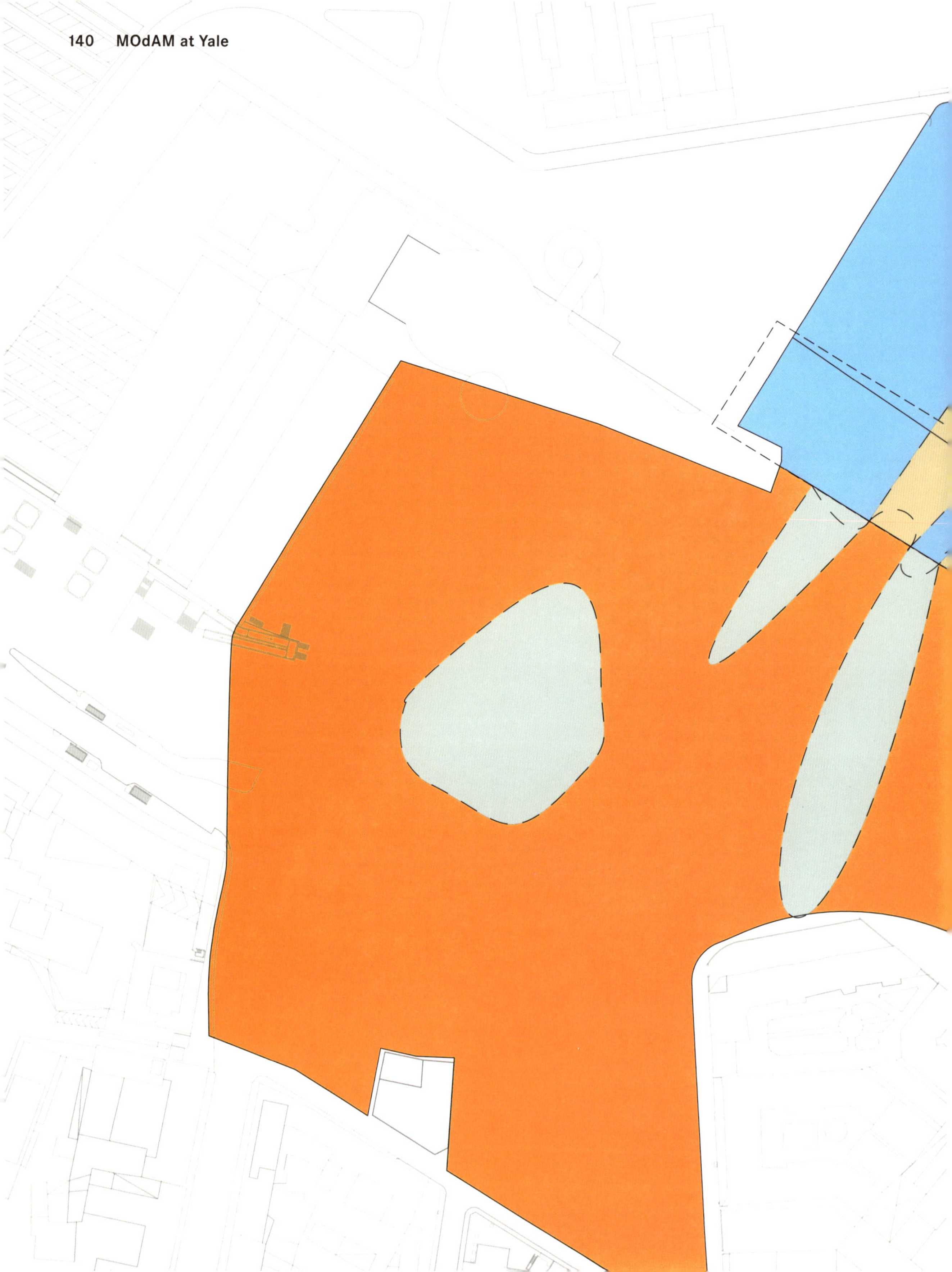

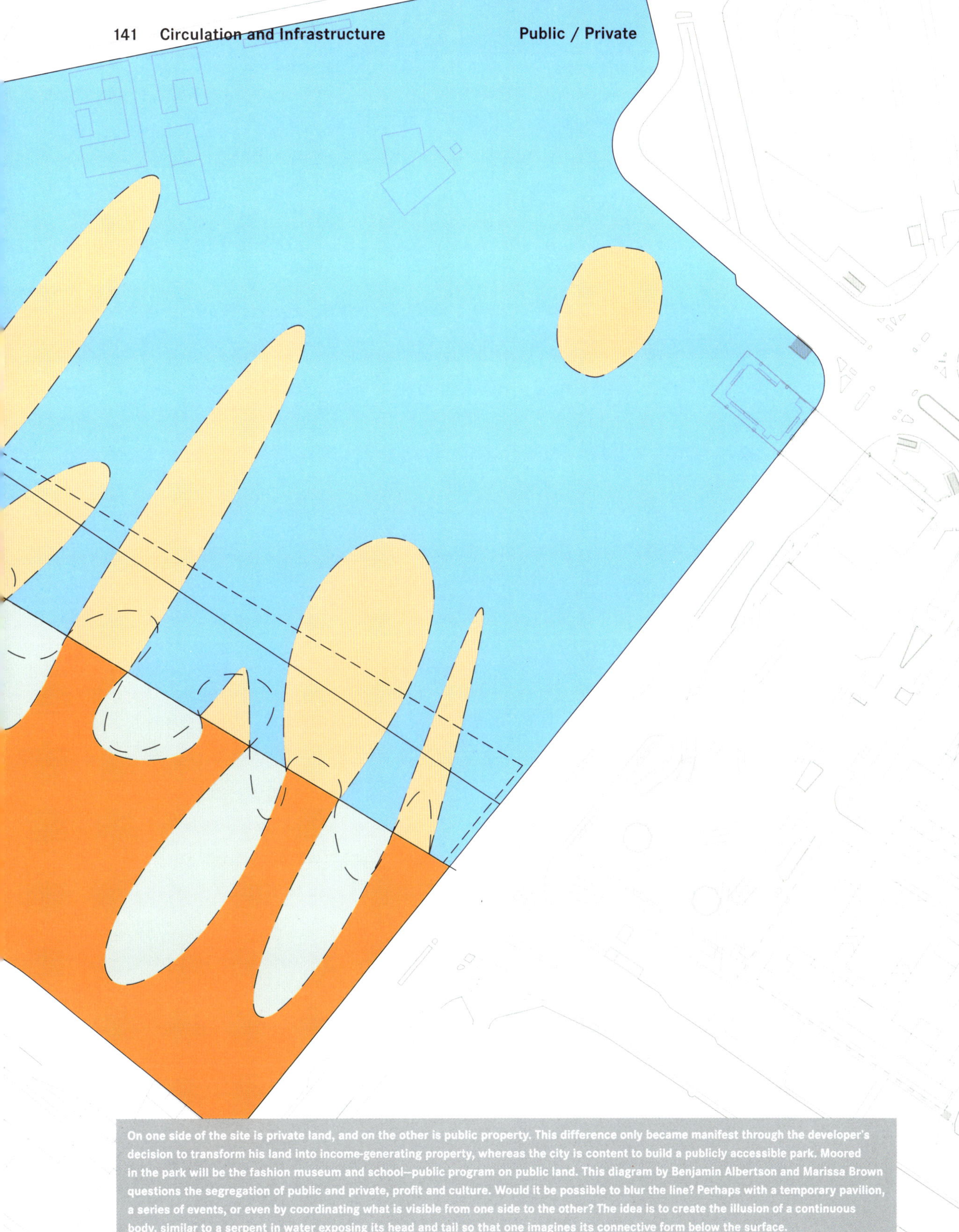

On one side of the site is private land, and on the other is public property. This difference only became manifest through the developer's decision to transform his land into income-generating property, whereas the city is content to build a publicly accessible park. Moored in the park will be the fashion museum and school—public program on public land. This diagram by Benjamin Albertson and Marissa Brown questions the segregation of public and private, profit and culture. Would it be possible to blur the line? Perhaps with a temporary pavilion, a series of events, or even by coordinating what is visible from one side to the other? The idea is to create the illusion of a continuous body, similar to a serpent in water exposing its head and tail so that one imagines its connective form below the surface.

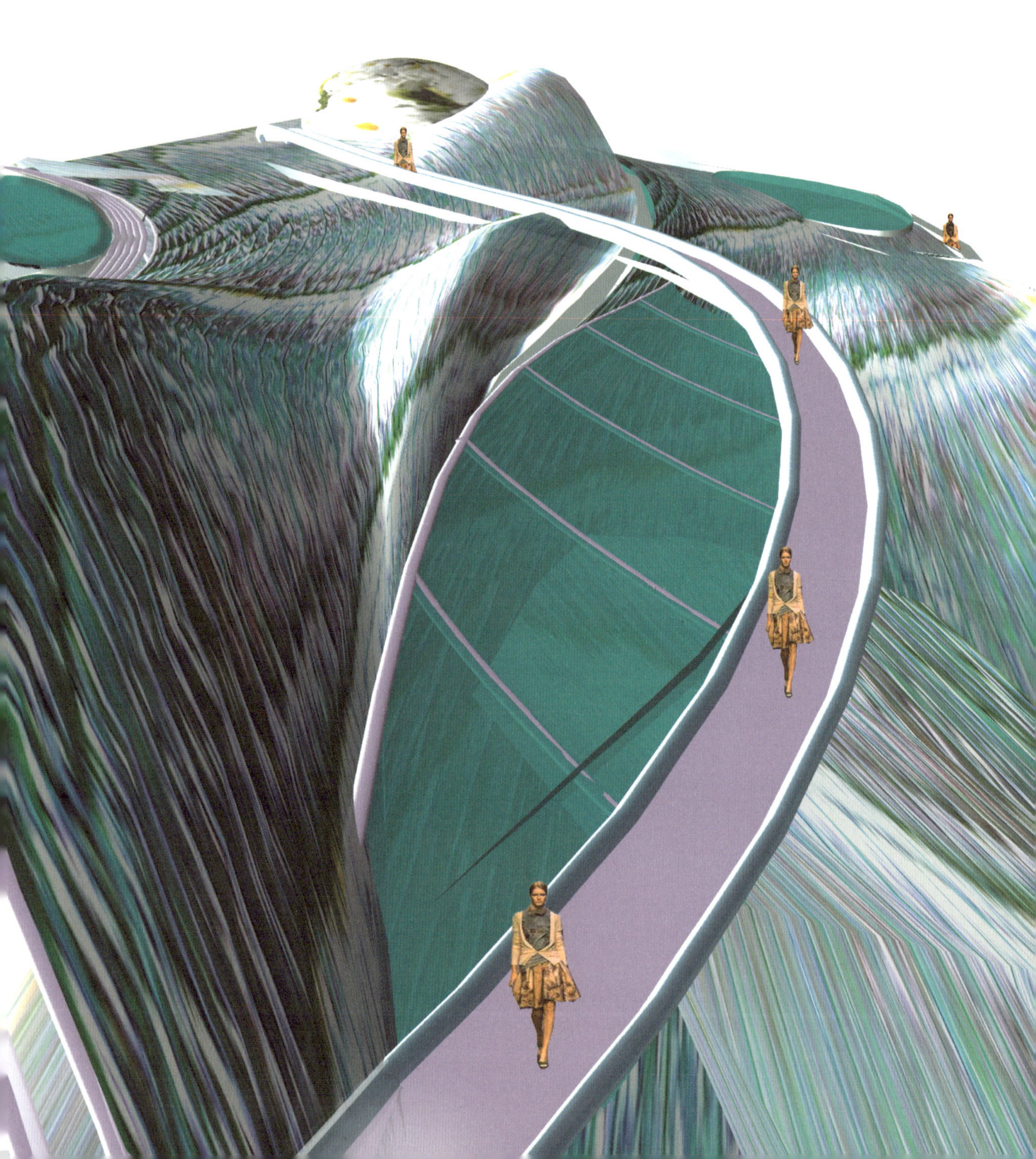

As discussed at the studio review of student Ceren Bingol:
Jay Wyper: It is amazing to me that you not only changed the master plan but had the time to go back and create an incredibly complex school and museum—and took it to the level that you did.

Gerald Hines: I think that the animation of the spaces is what we are trying to achieve and how you make things exciting for people to go through. You have created the idea of the animation, of drawing people in to be excited about the space they are in. And I think that's everything about the way architecture is going, in these urban spaces especially.

Brigitte Shim: You don't have to be visiting the museum to experience the building, but you can partake in it just by strolling in the neighborhood. And for me, that's a major armature of the project and that shouldn't be hidden. One of the strengths of the project is that it starts from a diagram and an idea that . . . the public is the structure which the programmatic elements are directly linked to. And then you can imagine how to apply structure and skin or any number of other issues to that piece of structure.

Perhaps that is how the runway show starts to happen. It doesn't actually happen in an internalized way. What is normally internalized becomes part of the public domain. It only happens twice a year, but it would be quite remarkable to imagine the building turning itself inside out. And the outside would be aware of what normally takes place inside.

opposite and next pages: Rendering of a public circulation spine over the MOdAM museum and school in the project of Ceren Bingol. The spine is an extension of the public space of the project.

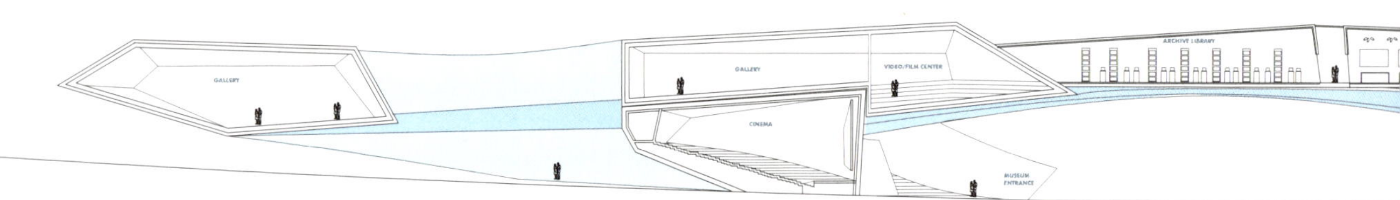
GALLERY
GALLERY
VIDEO/FILM CENTER
ARCHIVE LIBRARY
CINEMA
MUSEUM
ENTRANCE

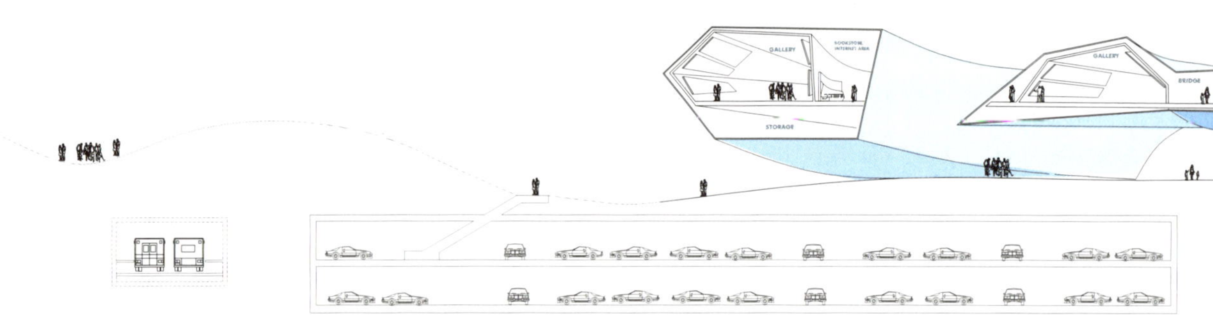
GALLERY
BOOKSTORE
INTERNET AREA
GALLERY
BRIDGE
STORAGE

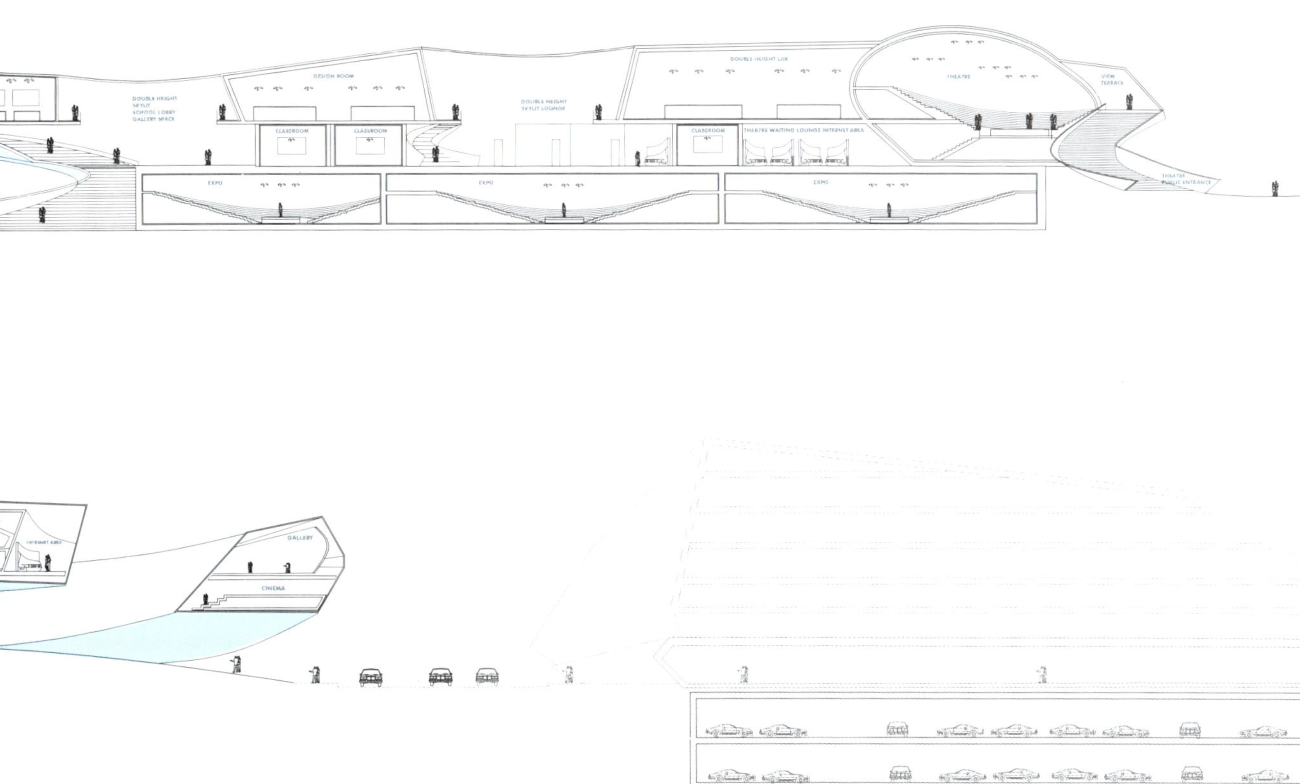
DOUBLE HEIGHT
SKYLIT
SCHOOL LOBBY
GALLERY SPACE
DESIGN ROOM
CLASSROOM
CLASSROOM
DOUBLE HEIGHT
SKYLIT LOUNGE
DOUBLE HEIGHT LAB
CLASSROOM
THEATRE WAITING LOUNGE INTERNET AREA
THEATRE
VIEW
TERRACE
THEATRE
PUBLIC ENTRANCE
EXPO
EXPO
EXPO
GALLERY
CINEMA

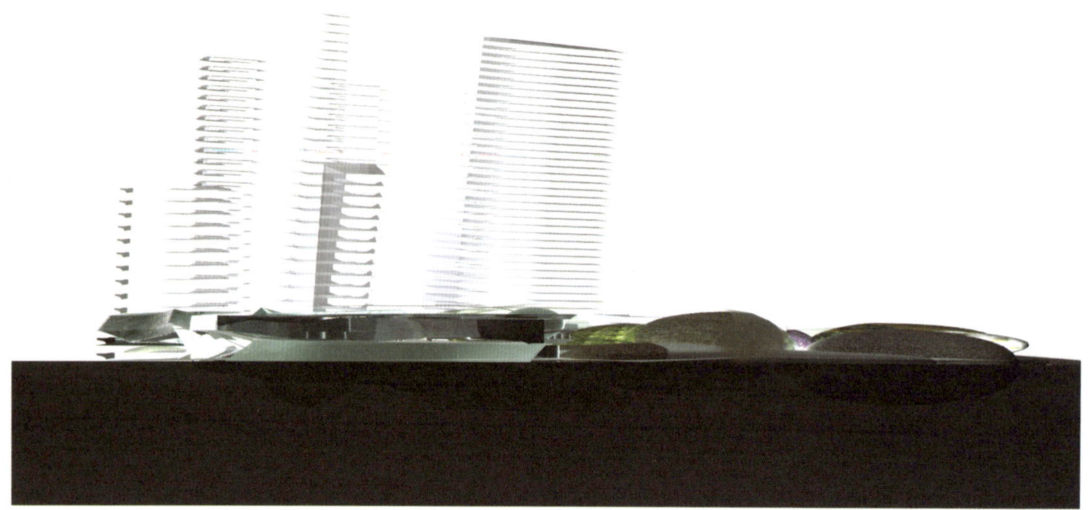

The opposition between a building and a landscape is never very firm, to the degree that it is possible to imagine near-total surrender of a building to its landscape. To conceive of a building as a landscape, as in the project by Ceren Bingol (above), requires not just continuity between inside and outside but a complete transformation of architectural design strategy, especially when it comes to the relationship between a building and its inhabitants. The design of circulation is key for the landscape-building. As the inside of a building becomes less a matter of floors and walls and more the arrangement of a topography or surfaces, architecture must release control over the movements and activities of the occupants. It is hard to wall off areas in a landscape; doors are a challenge, program slips and slides along the unbroken surfaces. Circulation is liberated but occupation is always provisional. Rather than a designated room for any given activity, the landscape has regions with qualities that are defined as much by the visitor as by the architect. Some areas are unexpectedly quiet—which would make for a good library—others are unintentionally busy. As in the student project by Benjamin Albertson and Marissa Brown (opposite), buildings are not so much architecture as they are infrastructure: resources to be utilized as a base of activities.

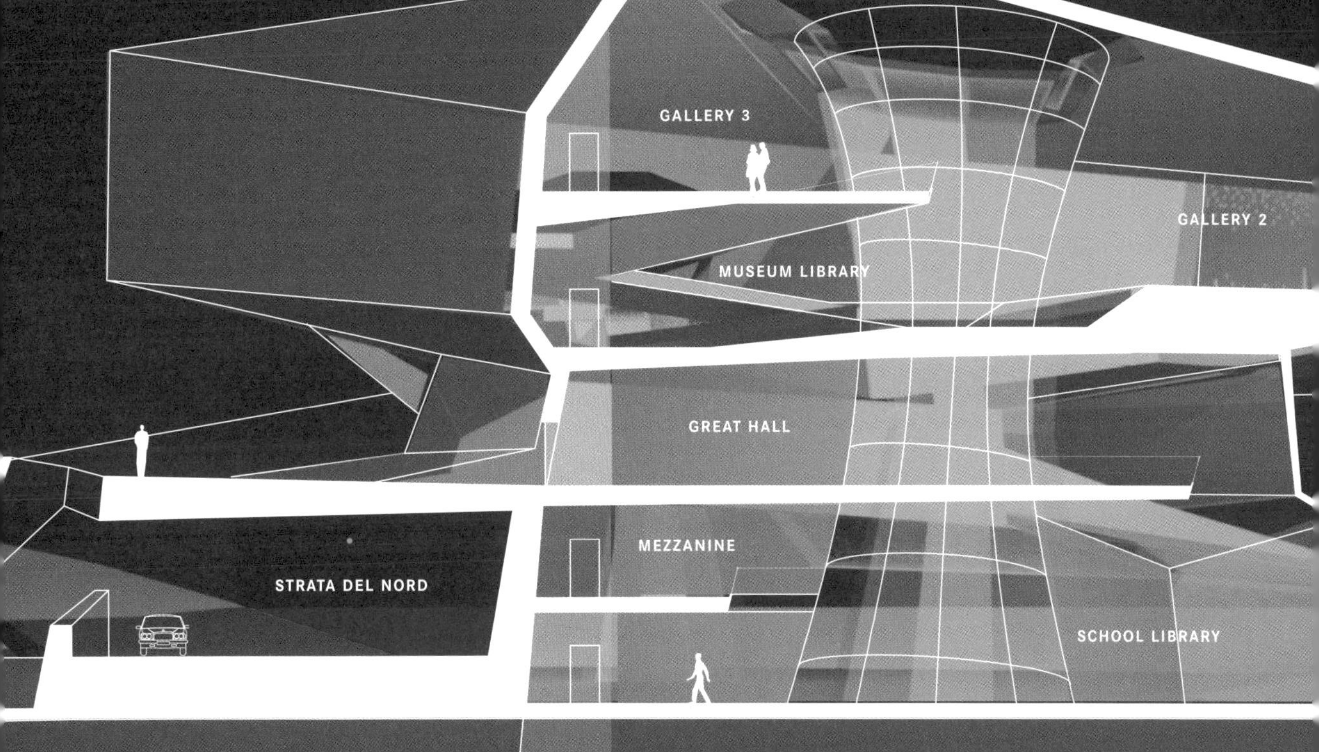
GALLERY 3
GALLERY 2
MUSEUM LIBRARY
GREAT HALL
MEZZANINE
STRATA DEL NORD
SCHOOL LIBRARY
PARKING

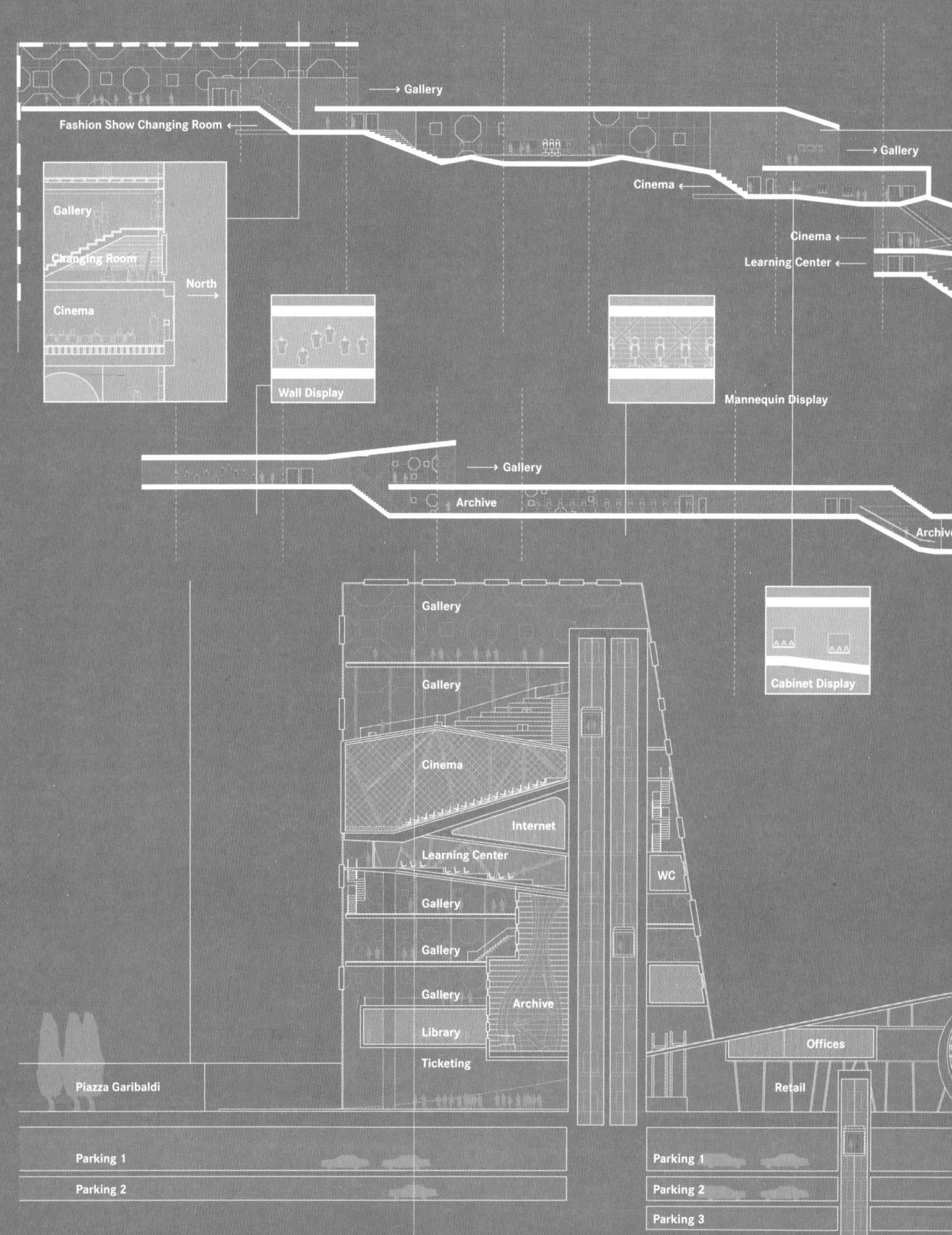
→ Gallery
Fashion Show Changing Room ←
→ Gallery
Cinema ←
Cinema ←
Learning Center ←
Gallery
Changing Room
North →
Cinema
Wall Display
Mannequin Display
→ Gallery
Archive
Archive
Cabinet Display
Gallery
Gallery
Cinema
Internet
Learning Center
WC
Gallery
Gallery
Gallery
Archive
Library
Ticketing
Offices
Retail
Piazza Garibaldi
Parking 1
Parking 2
Parking 1
Parking 2
Parking 3

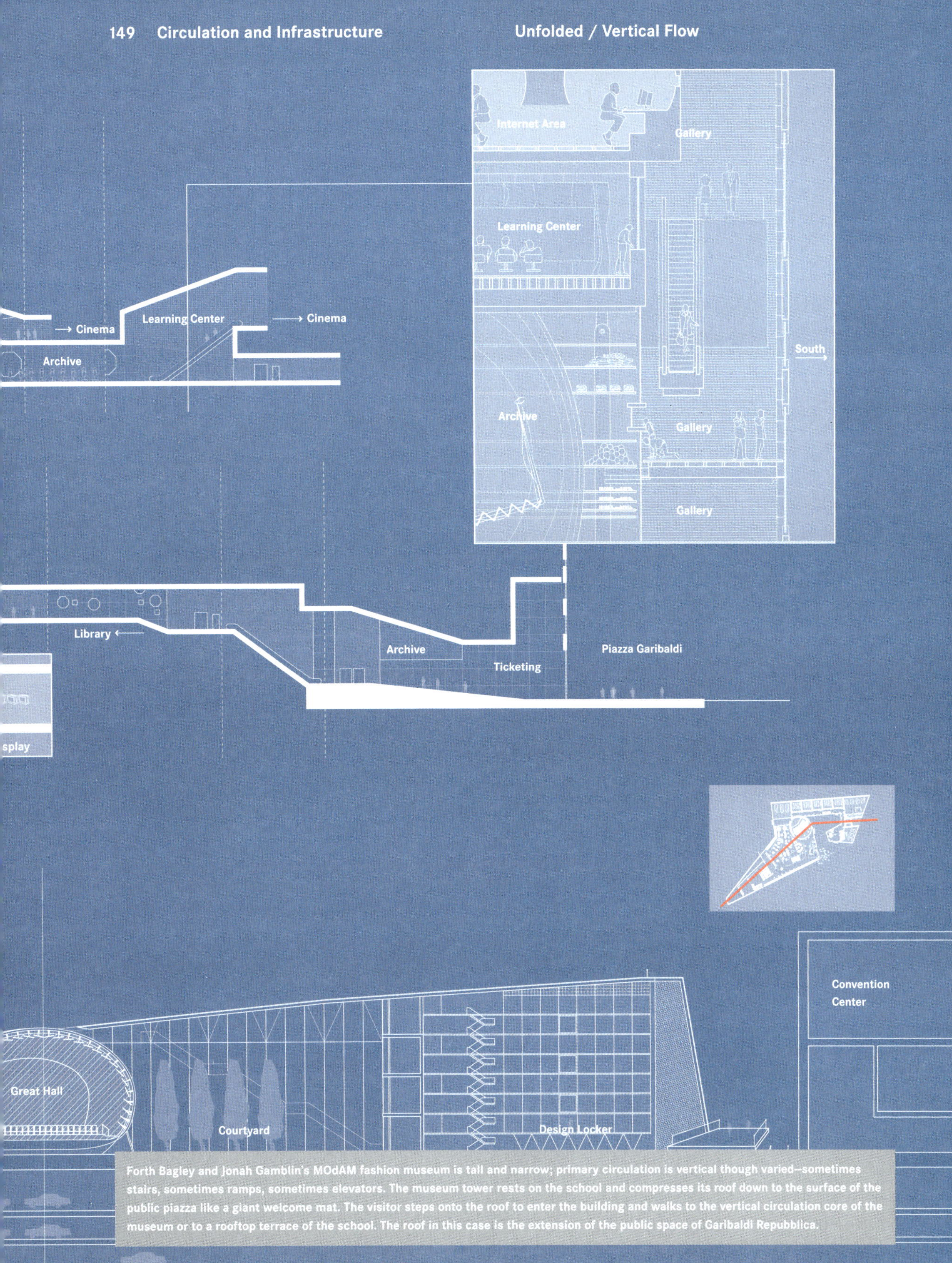

Forth Bagley and Jonah Gamblin's MOdAM fashion museum is tall and narrow; primary circulation is vertical though varied—sometimes stairs, sometimes ramps, sometimes elevators. The museum tower rests on the school and compresses its roof down to the surface of the public piazza like a giant welcome mat. The visitor steps onto the roof to enter the building and walks to the vertical circulation core of the museum or to a rooftop terrace of the school. The roof in this case is the extension of the public space of Garibaldi Repubblica.

Site Section

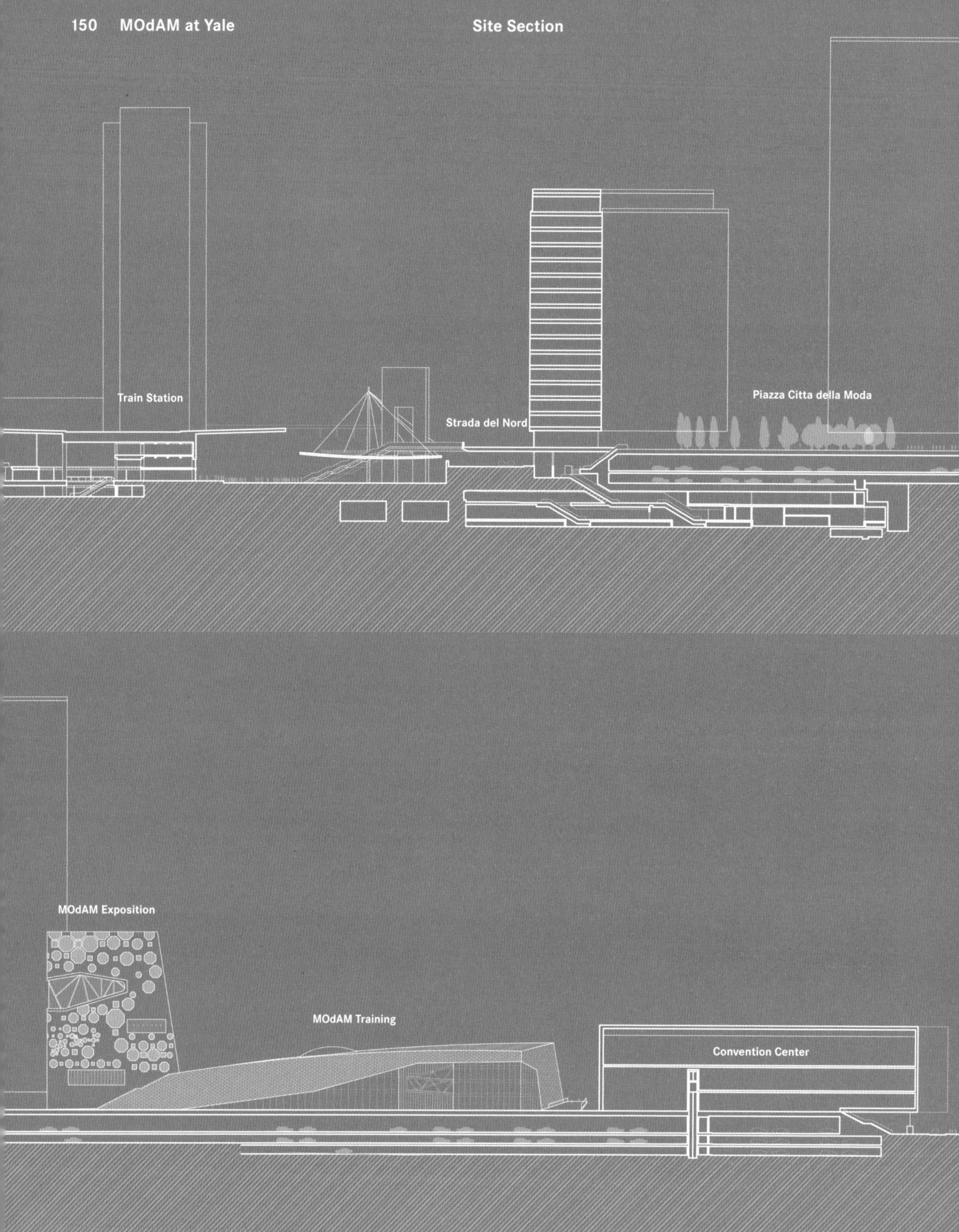

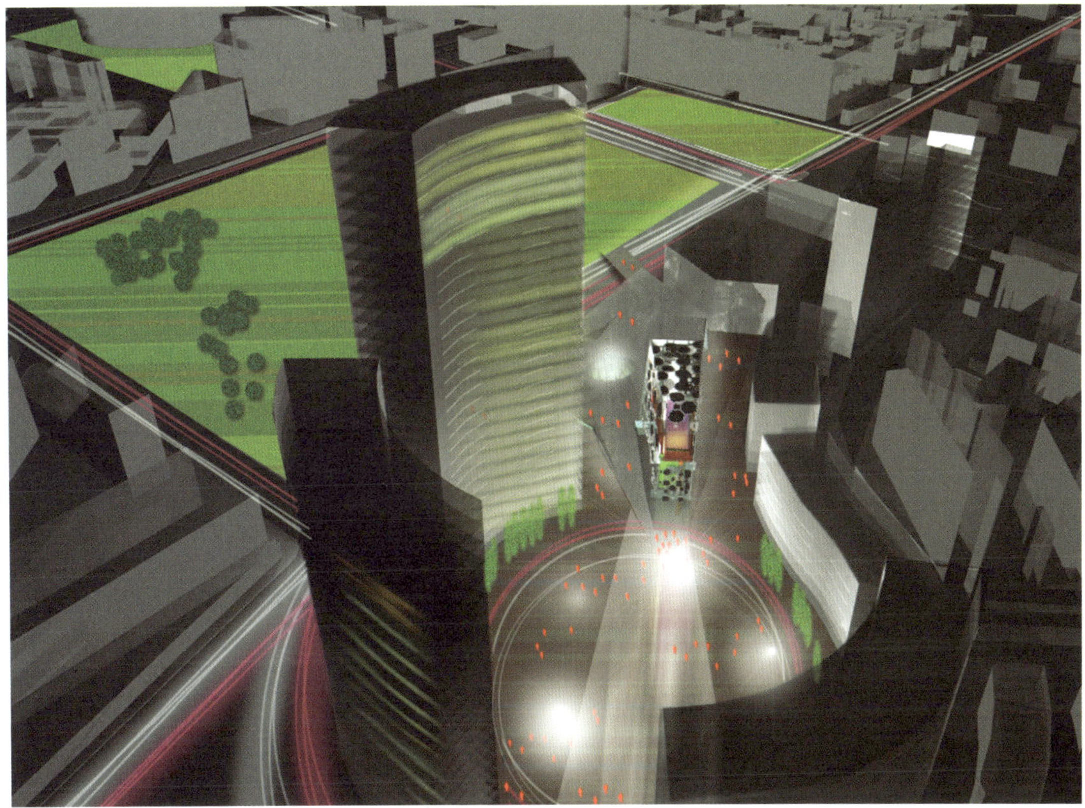

As discussed at the studio review of students Forth Bagley and Jonah Gamblin:
Jonah Gamblin: If we had one word to describe the project, it would be "proximity." Proximity for us has been a set of planning strategies, an architectural diagram; it has been an idea about fashion and fashion culture. It's a principle that if you take different things and you put them close enough together, you get something from the interaction that is more than the sum of its parts.

Henry Cobb: What makes it persuasive in terms of density is that the density is increased by a specifically public building—that is to say, a building that is accessible. So the idea that you could animate this new, very important space with a major iconic public building is valid. I think that covering roads in cities is very problematic, and I doubt very much that the traffic on this road is that different from any of the other roads to justify it being covered .... Again, I am going against, obviously, those who have been thinking about the park and the city and its relationship, but I think one bridge into the park is plenty.

opposite: Pelli Clark Pelli site section showing change in grade and circulation path from train station to Piazza Garibaldi and MOdAM. Connections to the subway lines from the piazza are also indicated.

above: Pelli Clark Pelli site rendering showing the vertical presence of MOdAM on the central piazza and the urban density generated by removing the canopy over Via del Nord and connecting the commercial development to the park.

Surface, Fashion, and Performance Enclosure

In the design of the fashion museum and school, the analogy between buildings and bodies was never far away. Research on fashion, textiles, and clothing design in the first weeks of the studio led to an awareness of the potential for exchange between fashion and architecture. In particular, it led to increased attention to building surfaces and how these surfaces join with or separate from other systems such as structure and circulation. Many projects approached the design of MOdAM like the design of a garment. Architecture resembled the work of weavers, pattern-makers, and tailors. Buildings were revealed through seams, stitching provided structure, column grids were woven, surfaces embroidered.

The influence of fashion was most evident in the design of cladding systems that often invoked the concept of a skin or responsive membrane enclosing the building, as seen in the following section. The drapes and folds of fabric first emulate then multiply and enhance human skin. Likewise, the architectural skins derived from fashion have an integral relationship to the underlying architecture. Unlike a conventional façade that can be isolated from the interior of a building, the qualities of a performance skin are determined by structural, programmatic, and environmental criteria. The skin can be seen as an index of the life of the building. It adjusts to occupational cycles: active and irregular at times, uniform and controlled at others. Like a garment, the skin responds to the activity of the body underneath, and it is the nature of that response, loose or tight, constricting or expansive, which produces the intended effects of style, performance, allure, or comfort.

above: Corrugated textile.

opposite: Haresh Lalvani, Waveknot, design made in conjunction with Milgo Bufkin fabricators for a folded metal architecture with algorithmically generated geometries, 2005.

2 Sheets—Sheet 1.

S. A. DREWRY.

Corset.

No. 237,503. **Patented Feb. 8, 1881.**

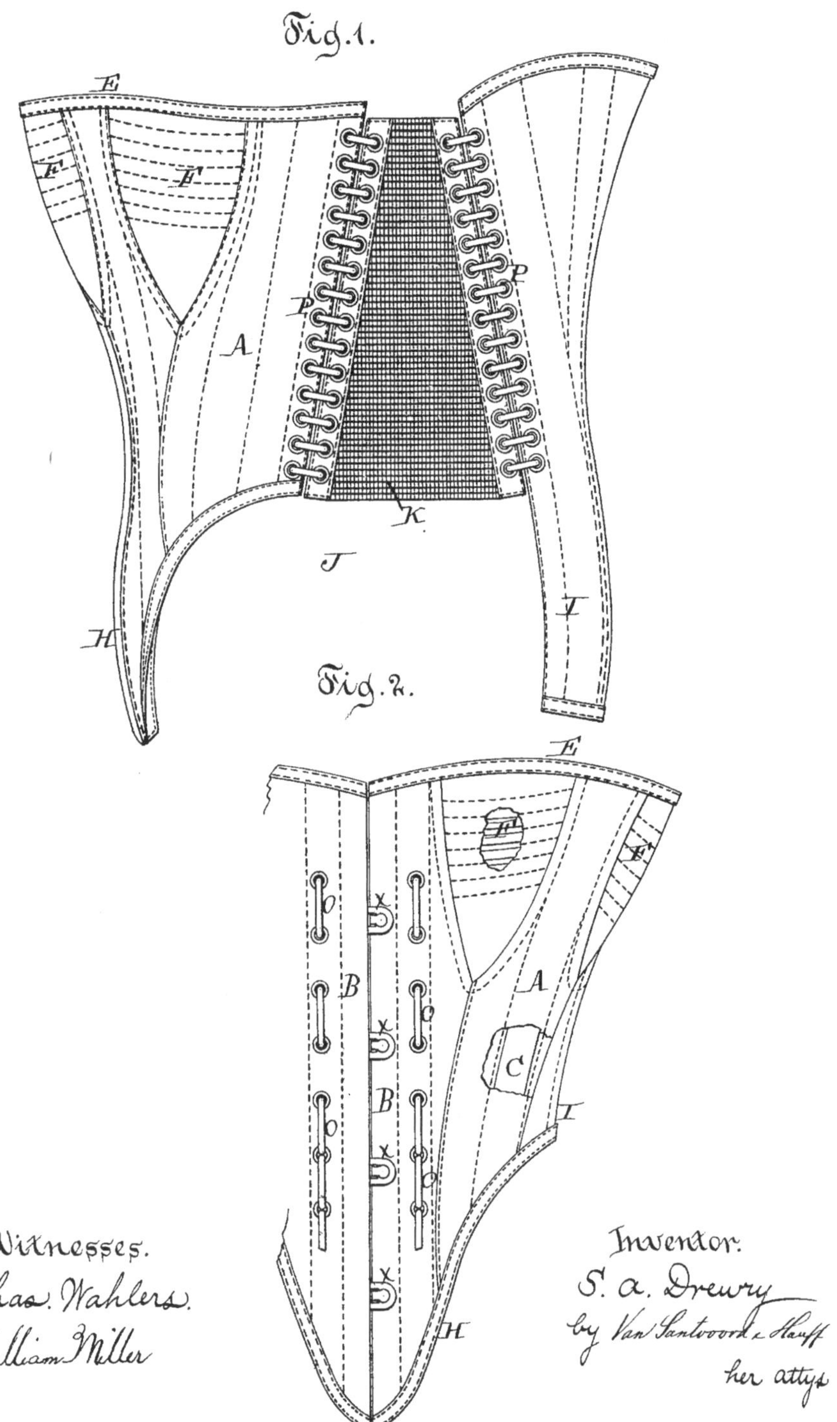

The corset molds the body to a supposed ideal, taking something soft and approximate and making it rigid and correct to realize the body through the garment and give it form. A similar principle is at work in the Seattle Public Library, although the dynamic between the soft internal and rigid external is much more ambiguous. The diagrid façade is structural—it carries some of the building load, unlike the ubiquitous free façade of most steel-and-glass buildings—but it is not the primary structural system of the building. Inside are program areas, each with a unique form determined by its use. For example, the book stack is a spiral that permits seamless growth or compression of the collection. The overall shape of the library is thus given by the organization of these program areas relative to one another—the reading room above the book spiral, etc. The façade wraps this organization and thus is able to carry load along the outside of the building; at the same time, however, it breaks free, inflating and producing large internal atriums, then suddenly fracturing, and cutting off space. The façade is both free from the body and still very dependent on it. And in this freedom to expand and to elaborate, coupled with need to support and constrict, the façade produces the iconic form of the building.

opposite: Patent application No. 237,503 for a corset, submitted by S. A. Drewry, February 8, 1881, page 1 of 2.
above: Office for Metropolitan Architecture, Seattle Public Library, Seattle, Washington, completed 2004. Gross Building Area: 412,000-square-feet

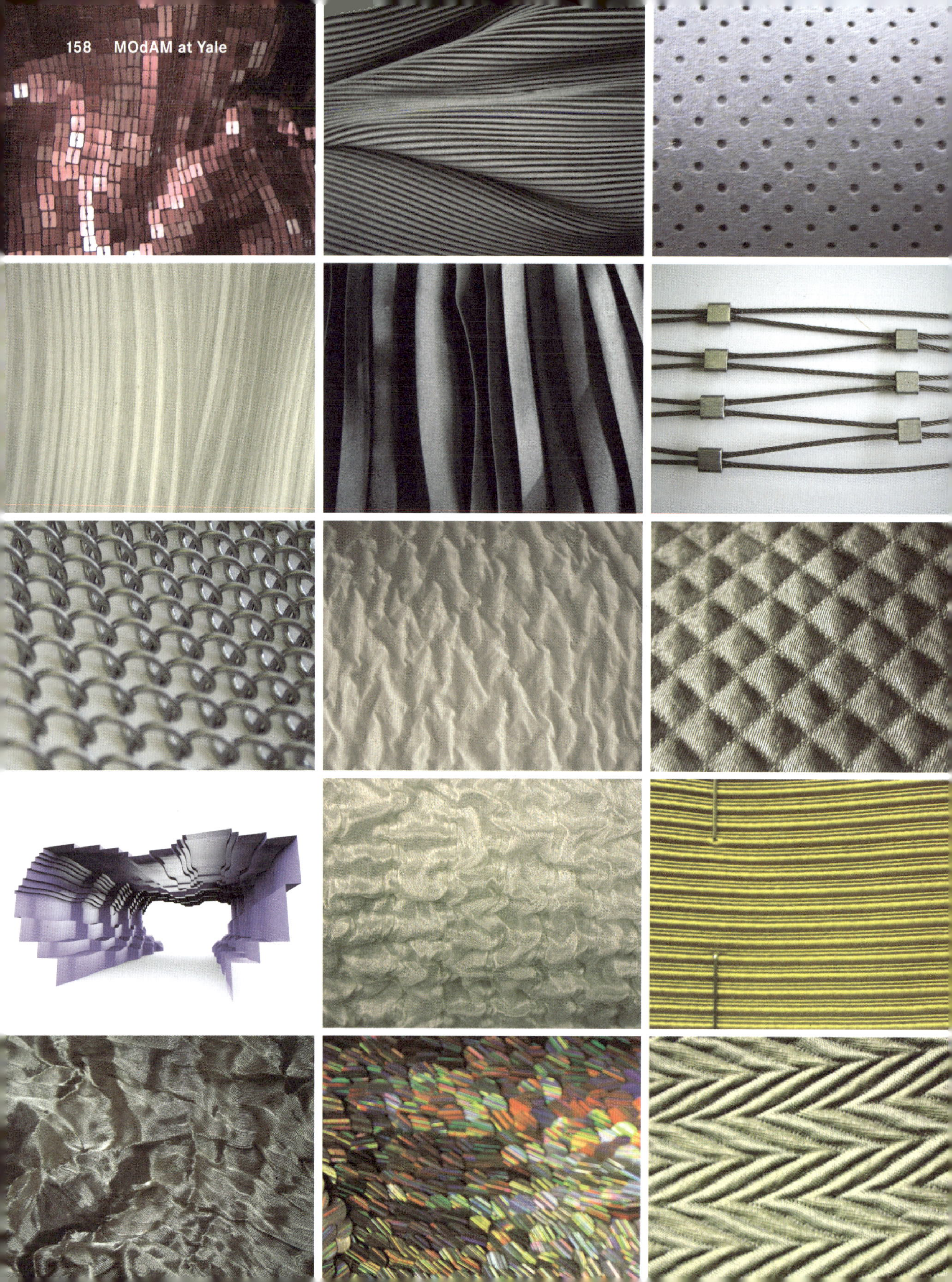

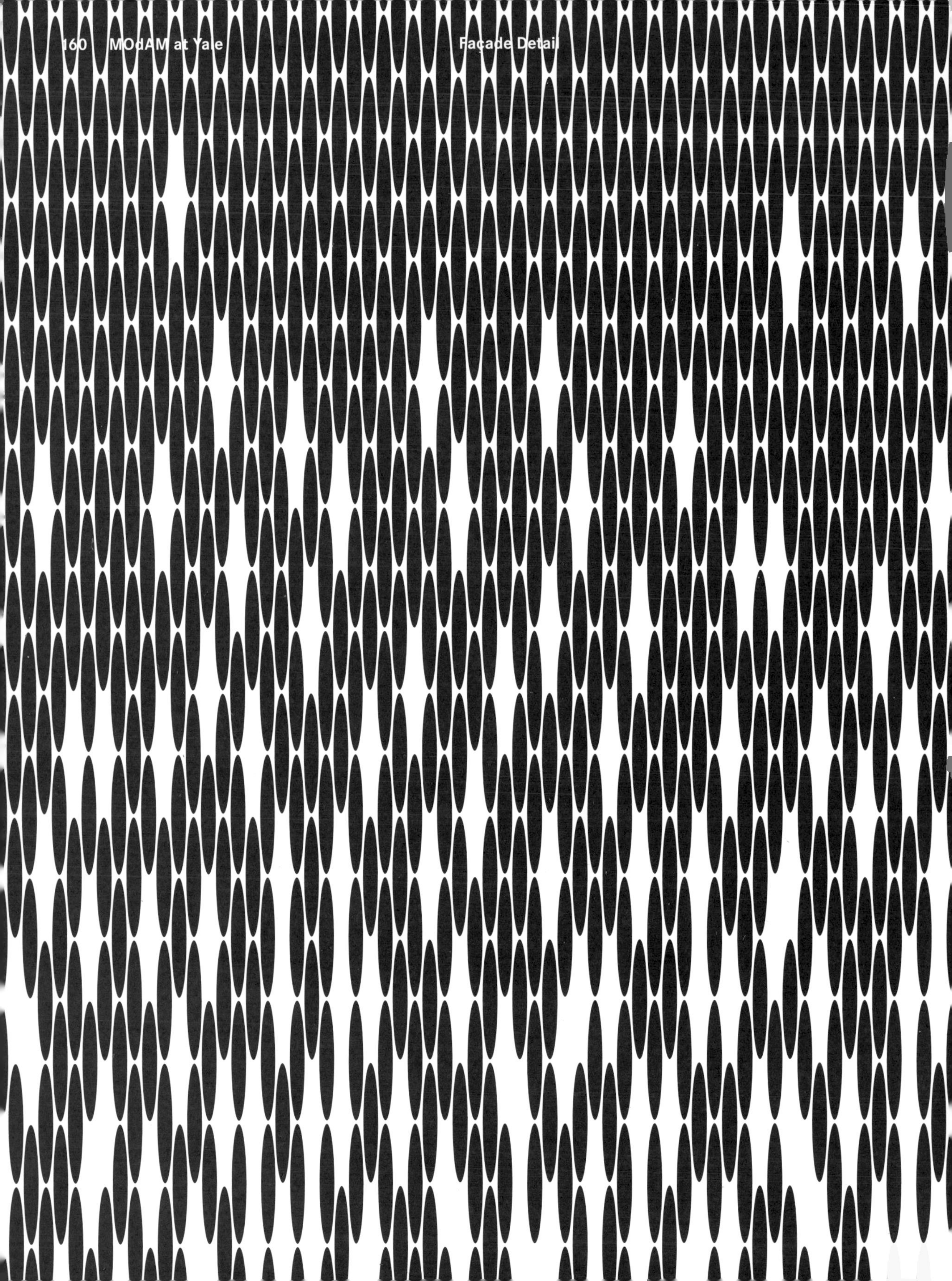

As discussed at the studio review of students Benjamin Albertson and Marissa Brown:
Robert Stern: No one has actually said whether they like your building or not. I think it's a very interesting building, and I think it is very well presented. I think that these questions are coming because people, when they are sympathetic, want to know more.

Mark Simon: I love that skin. Would you make it with sandblasting?

Cesar Pelli: It is very doable. If that is a pattern of mullions, you can in-fill each one with panels of a variety of materials.

Tod Williams: What are the elements that radiate between this building and the park and that mediate between your building and Pelli's master plan?

Rafael Viñoly: It seems to me that the most important thing in this project is the idea that it is much more of a virus that impregnates the whole thing, and to me that is programmatic.

Tod Williams: I agree but also think there should be a language of scalar elements that begins to deal with that on the outside. As much as I wanted the patterned skin to be continuous and whole, it does not have to invade everything.

Stefan Behnisch: I thought we could discuss whether it should be a building or not a building—I think that is a very valuable discussion in this context. I think the merits were when you started to work with the surface and created an architectural landscape with the park. I think the park and city are merging, and here it was merged in a good way. They developed out of that concept a building which has some stealth quality to it.

opposite: Benjamin Albertson and Marissa Brown's detail of the façade system, which is stretched over a rigid internal structure like a tensile net. Perforations are meant to invoke a worn fabric, with wear greater in regions of increased intensity produced by structural loads, internal circulation, or program.

above: Benjamin Albertson and Marissa Brown's template for a full architectural model showing each facet of the façade with perforations and fold lines for assembly.

above: The elevations of the five MOdAM buildings in the student project of Forth Bagley and Jonah Gamblin as generated by a sequence of computational algorithms that correspond to the organization of the primary structural system and desired opacity or transparency. The results of the algorithms are then color-coded by program and pixilated to produce patterns of perforation for daylight and ventilation.

opposite: The student project of Garo Balmanoukian diagrams the placement of octagonal "pillows" in the curtain-wall system relative to the programmatic organization of the MOdAM museum. The pillows function both as sunshades—and thus are more dense in areas that require controlled light—and as primary structural elements in the glass curtain-wall. Similar to a foam stiffener that absorbs vibrations in a tennis racket, the pillows cushion the façade against horizontal wind loads, allowing for the façade to take on an unbelievably light appearance: large white clouds floating in a glass sky.

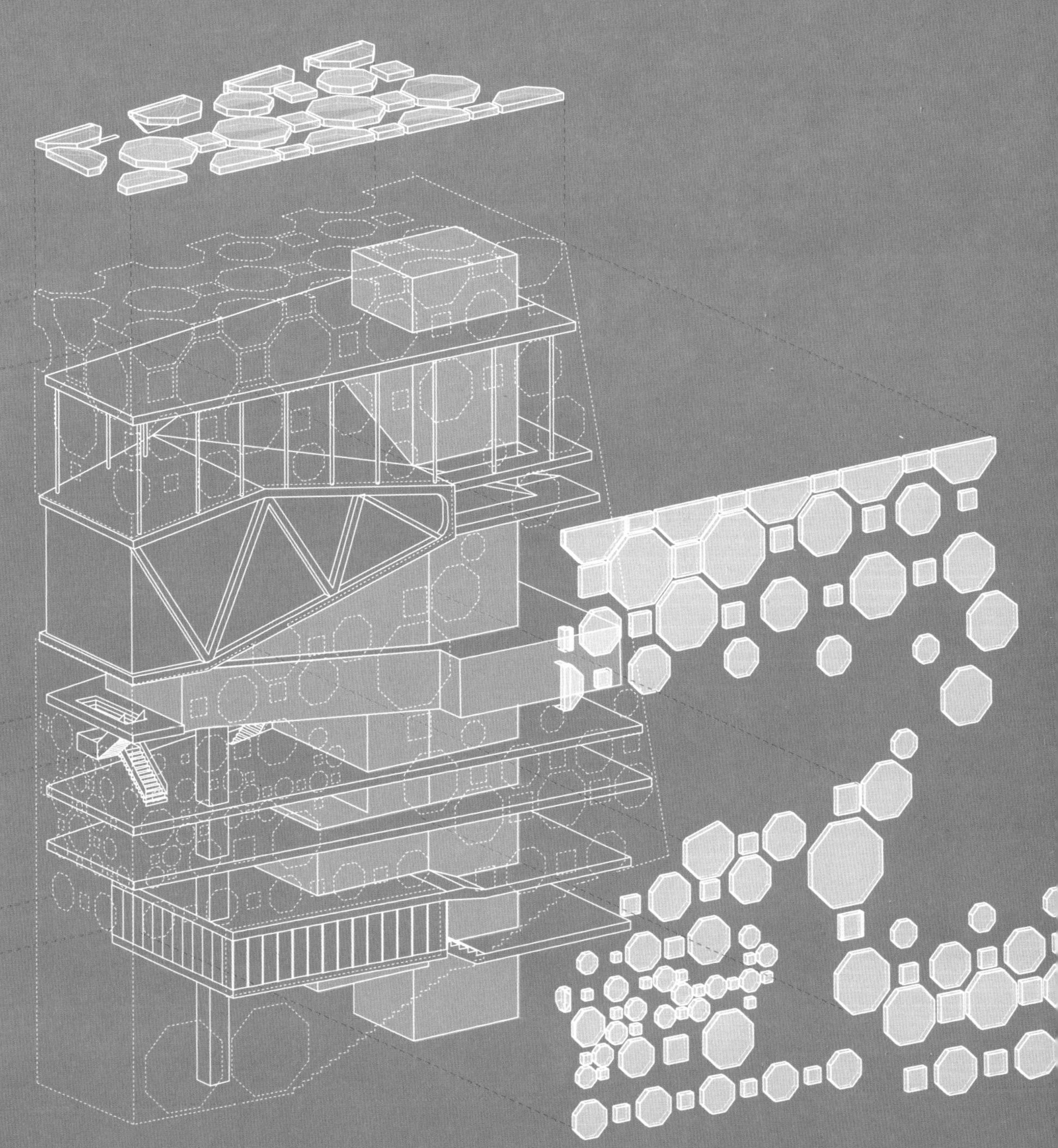

As discussed at the studio review of student Ceren Bingol:

Henry Cobb: The lizard skin is fascinating, and it makes me wonder about the relationship between fashion and architecture. In fashion, for environmental, aesthetic, and moral reasons, the use of animal skins is frowned upon. We no longer have alligator bags, fur collars, et cetera. Well, we're not supposed to have them. And I am wondering if, while fashion is pulling away from the natural and animal skins, architecture is moving toward them. And not just with your project; we're learning from the way nature has made skins.

Brigitte Shim: The whole area of bio-tech is really significant.

George Knight: Isn't it the case, specifically with lizard skin, that it's an incredibly complicated system based on the need of a lizard to move? The graphics even suggest that this building is actually moving. It looks as if you poked it, it might scoot over to the Piazza Garibaldi.

Rendering of student Ceren Bingol's building enclosure system. The shingles of the curtain wall mimic the formal and tectonic qualities of reptile skin. Detailing of the shingles permits use with any external formal geometry and constant adjustment of the internal qualities of the building. The skin is composed of opaque and transparent panels that are treated to provide a range of daylight levels or natural ventilation based on heat or cooling demands of the building.

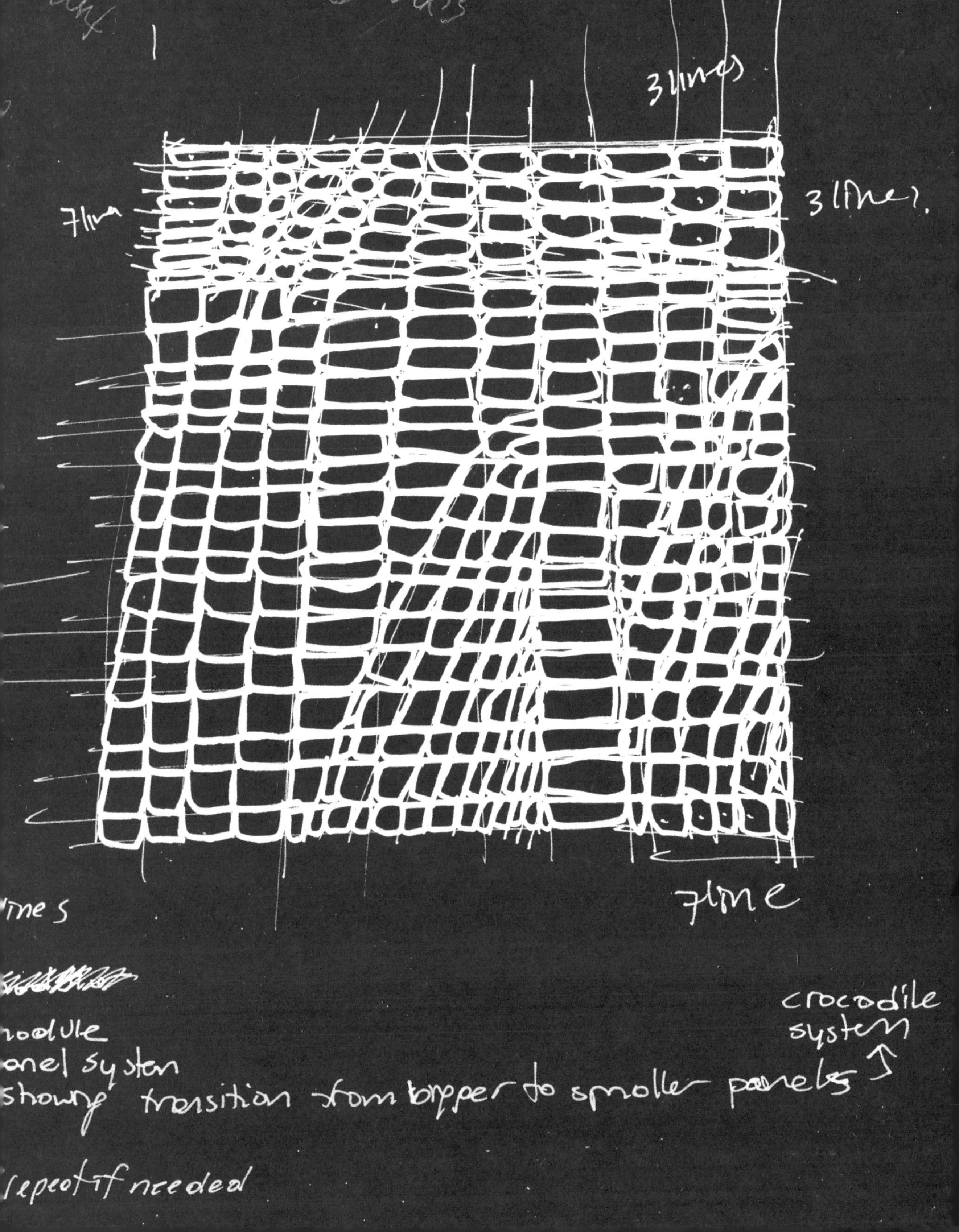

3 lines

7 line

3 lines.

7 line

ines

odule
anel system
showing transition from bigger to smaller panels

crocodile
system

repeat if needed

Style and Iconic Form

On the first day of the studio, Gerald Hines asked for an icon that, through architecture, would express Garibaldi Repubblica as a unique place and yet distinctly Milanese. For the developer of speculative real estate, the ability to establish the "right" architectural identity and to differentiate a project in a competitive property market is essential to its financial success. The importance of identity is all the greater when the project, like Garibaldi Repubblica, is at the scale of the city and must not only generate an architectural identity but establish that identity as a destination. The iconic quality of Garibaldi Repubblica was envisioned to be an entirely new place of great architectural design.

But what would make an icon in Milan today? Should the icon be radical and original, an unconventional set of buildings, a new mark on the skyline? Or perhaps, in keeping with Italian tradition, could Garibaldi Repubblica become iconic through its special role in the social life of the city? A spectrum emerged in the investigations of the studio, from formal experiments to how to promote a distinctly Milanese lifestyle of entertainment, nightlife, shopping, culture, and fashion through the architecture and public space of Garibaldi Repubblica. Student projects displayed the potential for a building's image to be absorbed into daily life through branding mechanisms of media and publicity. Media declares the project an icon publicly and iconographically by its pervasive visibility.

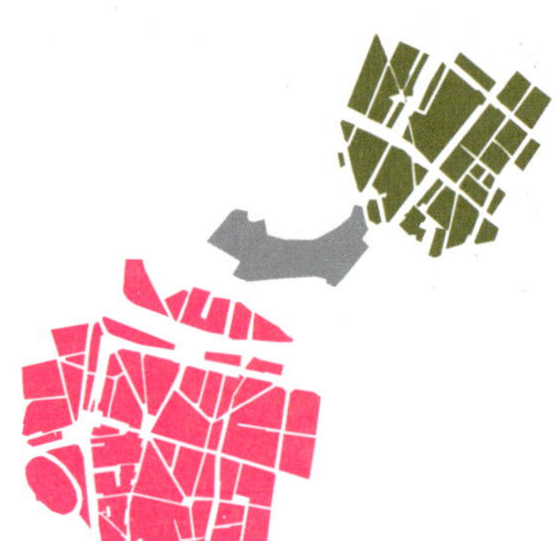

GARIBALDI REPUBBLICA (proposed)

BARS / RESTAURANTS / CLUBS

MOSCOVA Includes the Corso Garibaldi, which leads directly to the Corso Como, a pedestrian street that will be part of the Garibaldi Repubblica development.

NAVIGLI / PORTA TICINESE / PORTA GENOVA The neighborhood around the medieval city gate, in particular near the Colonne di San Lorenzo.

STAZIONE GARIBALDI/STAZIONE CENTRALE

VIA SAVONA

VIA CONCA DEL NAVIGLIO

PASSEGIATA The Galleria Vittorio Emanuele II and the pedestrian zones of the city along the Via Dante.

Shopping

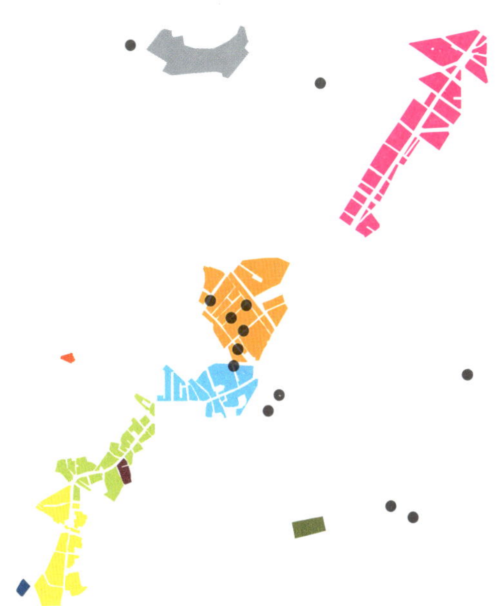

GARIBALDI REPUBBLICA (proposed)

STREETS

FASHION QUADRILATERO Around Via Montenapoleone, the center of high fashion and luxury in Milan.

CORSO VITTORIO EMMANUELE II Includes the Galleria on Piazza Duomo.

CORSO BUENOS AIRES Large department stores and flagship boutiques.

VIA TORINO Smaller boutiques for a younger demographic.

CORSO PORTA TICINESE The avant-garde of Milan fashion.

MARKETS

FIERA DI SINIGALLIA

LUNEDI DELL'ANGELO

MERCATO DEI FIORI

MERCATO DI VIA LORENZINI

● FASHION HOUSES The top twelve fashion houses in Milan, mainly located near the city's premier shopping area, the fashion *quadrilatero*.

Museums

6
7
4
3 1 2
5
8

GARIBALDI REPUBBLICA (proposed)

MODERN & CONTEMPORARY ART MUSEUMS

1 VILLA REALE AND CIVICA GALLERIA D'ARTE MODERNA
19th- and 20th-century Italian art.

2 CIVICO MUSEO D'ARTE CONTEMPORANEA (CIMAC)
20th-century art.

3 PADIGLIONE D'ARTE CONTEMPORANEA (PAC)
Temporary exhibitions of contemporary art.

SPECIAL INTEREST MUSEUMS

4 TRIENNALE DI MILANO

5 CIVICO MUSEO ARCHEOLOGICO

6 PALAZZO DUGNANI

7 MUSEO DI STORIA NATURALE

8 MUSEO NAZIONALE DELLA SCIENZA E DELLA TECNIA
'LEONARDO DA VINCI'

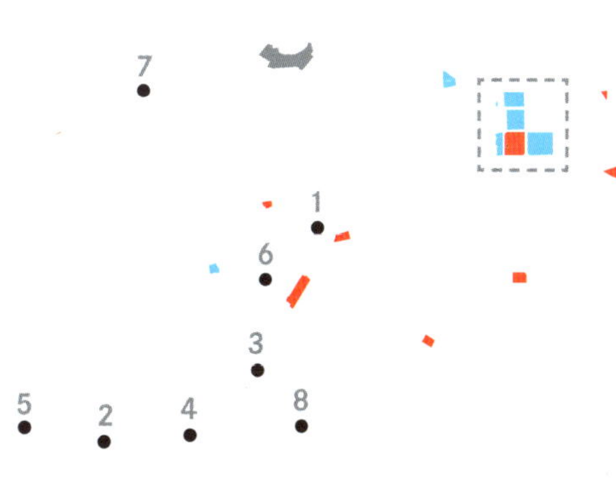

GARIBALDI REPUBBLICA (proposed)

UNIVERSITA DI MILANO

POLITECNICO DI MILANO

------ CITTA DEGLI STUDI The main student district in Milan and home to most of the city's university buildings.

1 ISTITUTO DI MODA BURGO

2 UNIVERSITA IULM

3 SDA BOCCONI

4 NOUVA ACCADEMIA DI BELLE ARTI

5 DOMUS ACADEMY

6 ISTITUTO ARTISTICO DELL'ABBLIGAMENTO "MARANGONI"

7 ISTITUTO CARTO SECOLI

8 ISTITUTO EUROPEO DI DESIGN

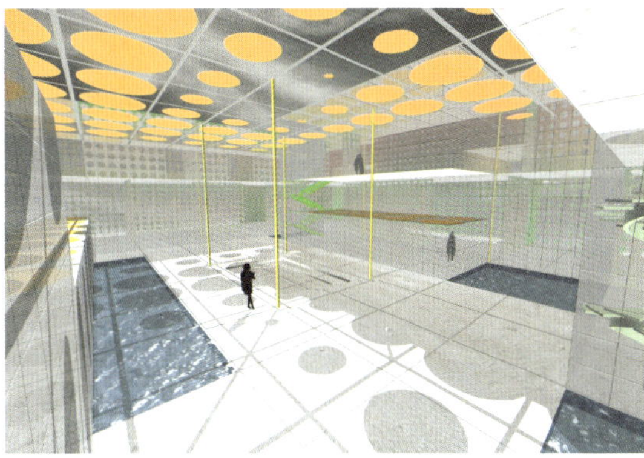

The icons of Milan, such as the Galleria Vittorio Emmanuel II or the Piazza Duomo, are not icons in the familiar sense of a visual marker for a city, like a symbolic tower or skyline; rather, they are landmarks because of the social and cultural activities that occur in them, as well as their historical and architectural significance.

Proposals for MOdAM identified the potential for a new icon of Milanese lifestyle at Garibaldi Repubblica. Fashion will define the experience—a culture of display, of communication, of an international, media-rich synthesis of styles and influences. The role of architecture in this experience, however, was conceived in many ways, as in the projects by Ceren Bingol (opposite and previous); Forth Bagley and Jonah Gamblin (above, top row); and Genevieve Fu and Brett Spearman (above, middle and bottom rows). The building may be like a catalog of objects put together in a set of highly specific environments or, conversely, an extended experience woven together gradually over different levels, ramps, and galleries.

If, according to Coco Chanel, "fashion is architecture," then today the influence of a handful of international architects in popular culture and the growing awareness of the marketability of that influence threatens to render architecture as fashion. As the brand names in the fashion industry are used to sell a lifestyle through a handbag or pair of sunglasses, developers are beginning to realize the premium value of name-brand architecture. New residential developments offer the design services of a Richard Meier or Charles Gwathmey as the ultimate luxury; museums use a new lobby by, say, Santiago Calatrava or an extension by Renzo Piano to lure more visitors, first for the building and then for the art. Fashion itself has also begun to capitalize on the selling power of architects, as in Prada's "epicenters" (by Rem Koolhaas and Herzog & de Meuron) or Issey Miyake's New York boutique (by Frank Gehry).

As architecture, like fashion, becomes increasingly perceived as a lifestyle product, architects have the opportunity to consider the design of this lifestyle as much a part of a building as its physical architecture. For the Citta della Moda, the success of the project as a speculative development depends on the ability of the architects and developers to cultivate a certain perception. Identity can be added to form and function as basic criteria for the architecture. Image is key, but which image is right? What does a city of fashion look like? How does one live or work there? What is the lifestyle, and how can architecture stimulate our desire for it?

Collage images by Forth Bagley and Jonah Gamblin.

Milan's MOdAM

FASHION AS AF

la Repubblica

I terroristi dirottano quattro voli di linea, rase al suolo le Torri gemelle di Manhattan. Chiusi tutti gli aeroporti Usa

Ecco il Nouvo Milano

Il nouvo Milano alla Stazione Garribaldi Repubblica

L'OCCIDENTE COLPITO AL CUORE

La Moda di Milano

STEPHEN KING

L'ACCHIAPPASOGNI

The Economist

Privacy under threat - voluntarily
PAGE 16-30

Latin Americans prefer democrac
PAGE 40-42

Health care for the poor world
PAGE 44-45

AUGUST 17TH-23RD 2006

Review and Studio Discussion

Studio review jury from top clockwise: George Knight (with coffee cup), Mark Simon, Gerald Hines, Rafael Viñoly, Cesar Pelli, Robert A. M. Stern (pointing), Stefan Behnisch (standing), Harry Cobb (seated), Jay Wyper (seated), and Tod Williams (white T-shirt).

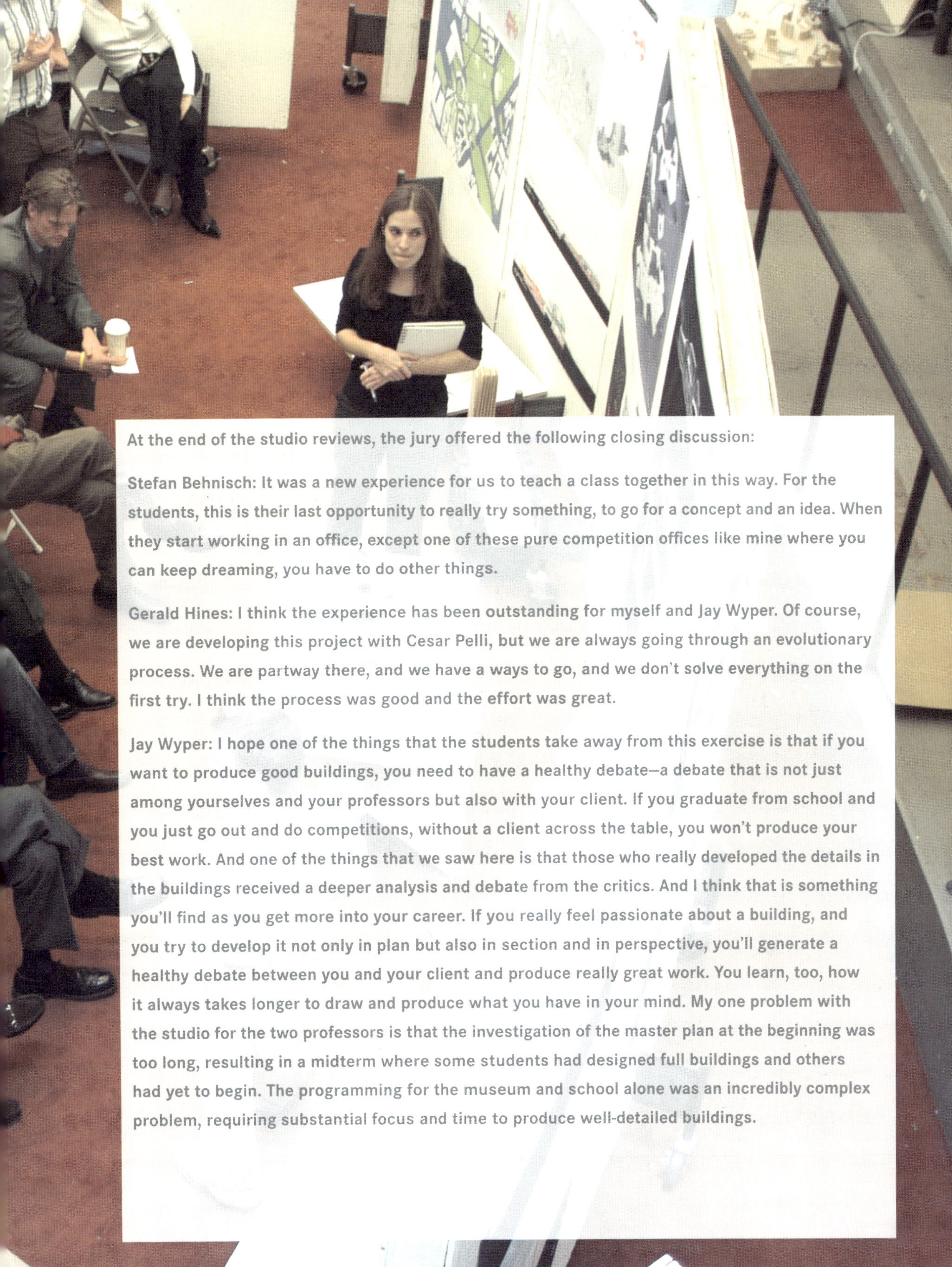

At the end of the studio reviews, the jury offered the following closing discussion:

Stefan Behnisch: It was a new experience for us to teach a class together in this way. For the students, this is their last opportunity to really try something, to go for a concept and an idea. When they start working in an office, except one of these pure competition offices like mine where you can keep dreaming, you have to do other things.

Gerald Hines: I think the experience has been outstanding for myself and Jay Wyper. Of course, we are developing this project with Cesar Pelli, but we are always going through an evolutionary process. We are partway there, and we have a ways to go, and we don't solve everything on the first try. I think the process was good and the effort was great.

Jay Wyper: I hope one of the things that the students take away from this exercise is that if you want to produce good buildings, you need to have a healthy debate—a debate that is not just among yourselves and your professors but also with your client. If you graduate from school and you just go out and do competitions, without a client across the table, you won't produce your best work. And one of the things that we saw here is that those who really developed the details in the buildings received a deeper analysis and debate from the critics. And I think that is something you'll find as you get more into your career. If you really feel passionate about a building, and you try to develop it not only in plan but also in section and in perspective, you'll generate a healthy debate between you and your client and produce really great work. You learn, too, how it always takes longer to draw and produce what you have in your mind. My one problem with the studio for the two professors is that the investigation of the master plan at the beginning was too long, resulting in a midterm where some students had designed full buildings and others had yet to begin. The programming for the museum and school alone was an incredibly complex problem, requiring substantial focus and time to produce well-detailed buildings.

above, clockwise from top right: Markus Dochantschi, Jay Wyper and Gerald Hines, Rafael Viñoly, and Greg Lynn.

opposite: Stefan Behnisch

Markus Dochantschi: I think the students were very positive about having two processes run parallel: The process of investigating ideas that are abstract and not buildable while at the same time working to produce a concrete, sustainable building—to think simultaneously about their responsibility as an architect and their responsibility as an urban planner in Milan. Every student had the opportunity to say, "Okay, we can work with the Pelli Master Plan, manipulate it or start from scratch." Harry Cobb asked, "Why did you have to work on the plan in that way?" The response, from a planning perspective, is that it was based on the requirements of the city. From the perspective of an architect, the answer is completely different. I think it was good to give students the opportunity to challenge the established plan, to throw it out and be forced to consider all the complex set of concerns—from the city, from the public, and from the developers—which go into this project. The students also had the benefit of going through this process with a very experienced and very educated client in Gerry and Jay.

Jay Wyper: What the city wants is an iconic building in the park to center this place. If somebody were to follow that logic and design—not the building—but to put the position here and then say, "By the way, in designing this building we really thought that *this* in the master plan had to change for the following reasons," that would be very valid. But rather than spend so much effort re-master-planning this place—and I agree, there are weaknesses to it—but the class so far has come up with a lot of good ideas that we will take back to the Pelli firm and talk about. Your job is to design these buildings. And I guarantee you, it is a really tough program. As you have thought about the front door, the back door, private space, open space, you have a lot of good analysis. Designing the MOdAM building raises a whole lot of issues that you worked to resolve in the master plan, but the way to do it is through [an actual] building. As Robert Stern previously noted to the students, there are a lot of compromises in the master plan, and you know half of them, but you don't know the other half. The master plan is like this for a reason, and we made certain decisions and other trade-offs. But when designing the building, how do you design an iconic building with the towers in the master plan there? You had to resolve that. This tower is not going away. You had to figure out how to make this an iconic building by itself.

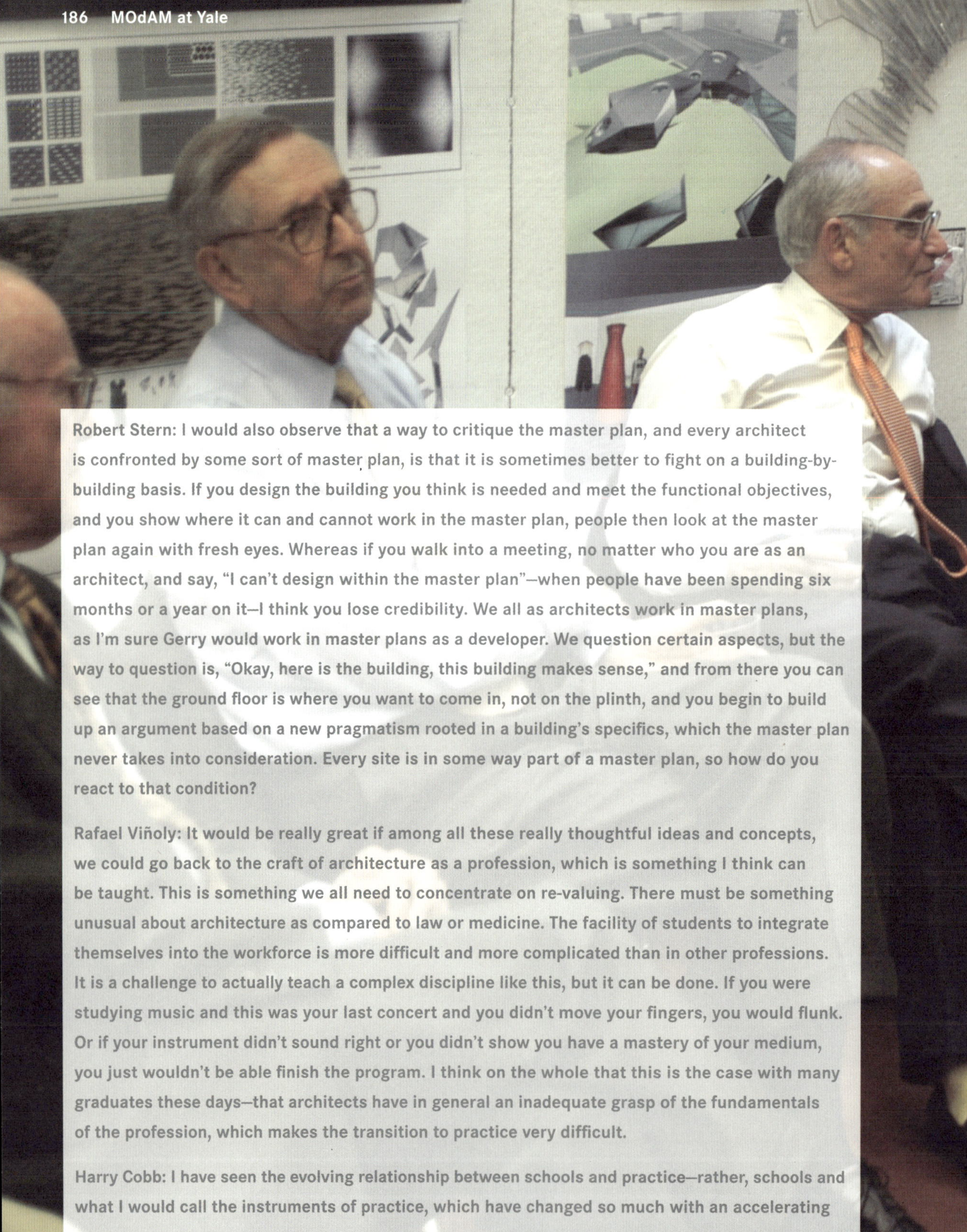

Robert Stern: I would also observe that a way to critique the master plan, and every architect is confronted by some sort of master plan, is that it is sometimes better to fight on a building-by-building basis. If you design the building you think is needed and meet the functional objectives, and you show where it can and cannot work in the master plan, people then look at the master plan again with fresh eyes. Whereas if you walk into a meeting, no matter who you are as an architect, and say, "I can't design within the master plan"—when people have been spending six months or a year on it—I think you lose credibility. We all as architects work in master plans, as I'm sure Gerry would work in master plans as a developer. We question certain aspects, but the way to question is, "Okay, here is the building, this building makes sense," and from there you can see that the ground floor is where you want to come in, not on the plinth, and you begin to build up an argument based on a new pragmatism rooted in a building's specifics, which the master plan never takes into consideration. Every site is in some way part of a master plan, so how do you react to that condition?

Rafael Viñoly: It would be really great if among all these really thoughtful ideas and concepts, we could go back to the craft of architecture as a profession, which is something I think can be taught. This is something we all need to concentrate on re-valuing. There must be something unusual about architecture as compared to law or medicine. The facility of students to integrate themselves into the workforce is more difficult and more complicated than in other professions. It is a challenge to actually teach a complex discipline like this, but it can be done. If you were studying music and this was your last concert and you didn't move your fingers, you would flunk. Or if your instrument didn't sound right or you didn't show you have a mastery of your medium, you just wouldn't be able finish the program. I think on the whole that this is the case with many graduates these days—that architects have in general an inadequate grasp of the fundamentals of the profession, which makes the transition to practice very difficult.

Harry Cobb: I have seen the evolving relationship between schools and practice—rather, schools and what I would call the instruments of practice, which have changed so much with an accelerating

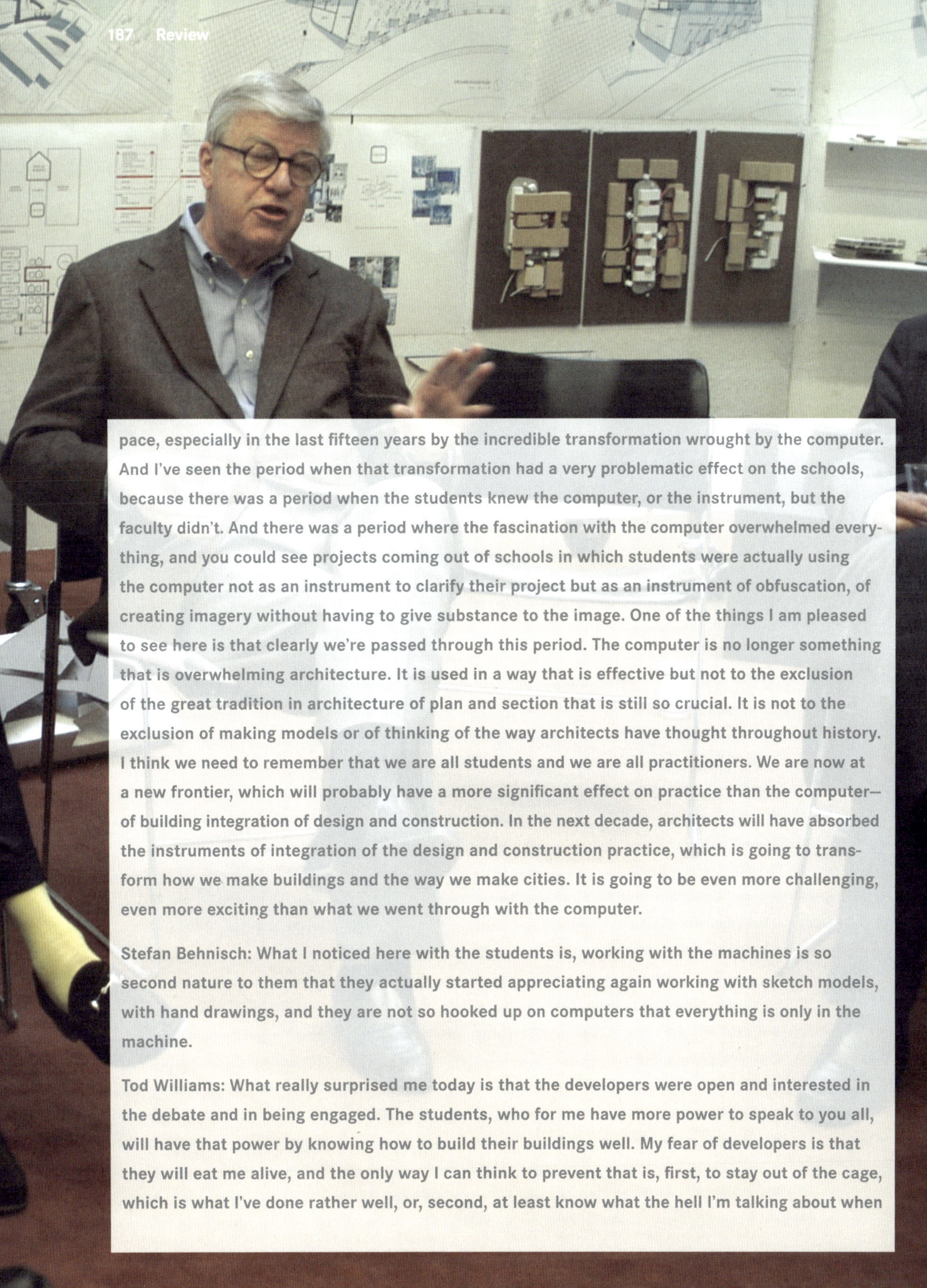

pace, especially in the last fifteen years by the incredible transformation wrought by the computer. And I've seen the period when that transformation had a very problematic effect on the schools, because there was a period when the students knew the computer, or the instrument, but the faculty didn't. And there was a period where the fascination with the computer overwhelmed everything, and you could see projects coming out of schools in which students were actually using the computer not as an instrument to clarify their project but as an instrument of obfuscation, of creating imagery without having to give substance to the image. One of the things I am pleased to see here is that clearly we're passed through this period. The computer is no longer something that is overwhelming architecture. It is used in a way that is effective but not to the exclusion of the great tradition in architecture of plan and section that is still so crucial. It is not to the exclusion of making models or of thinking of the way architects have thought throughout history. I think we need to remember that we are all students and we are all practitioners. We are now at a new frontier, which will probably have a more significant effect on practice than the computer—of building integration of design and construction. In the next decade, architects will have absorbed the instruments of integration of the design and construction practice, which is going to transform how we make buildings and the way we make cities. It is going to be even more challenging, even more exciting than what we went through with the computer.

Stefan Behnisch: What I noticed here with the students is, working with the machines is so second nature to them that they actually started appreciating again working with sketch models, with hand drawings, and they are not so hooked up on computers that everything is only in the machine.

Tod Williams: What really surprised me today is that the developers were open and interested in the debate and in being engaged. The students, who for me have more power to speak to you all, will have that power by knowing how to build their buildings well. My fear of developers is that they will eat me alive, and the only way I can think to prevent that is, first, to stay out of the cage, which is what I've done rather well, or, second, at least know what the hell I'm talking about when

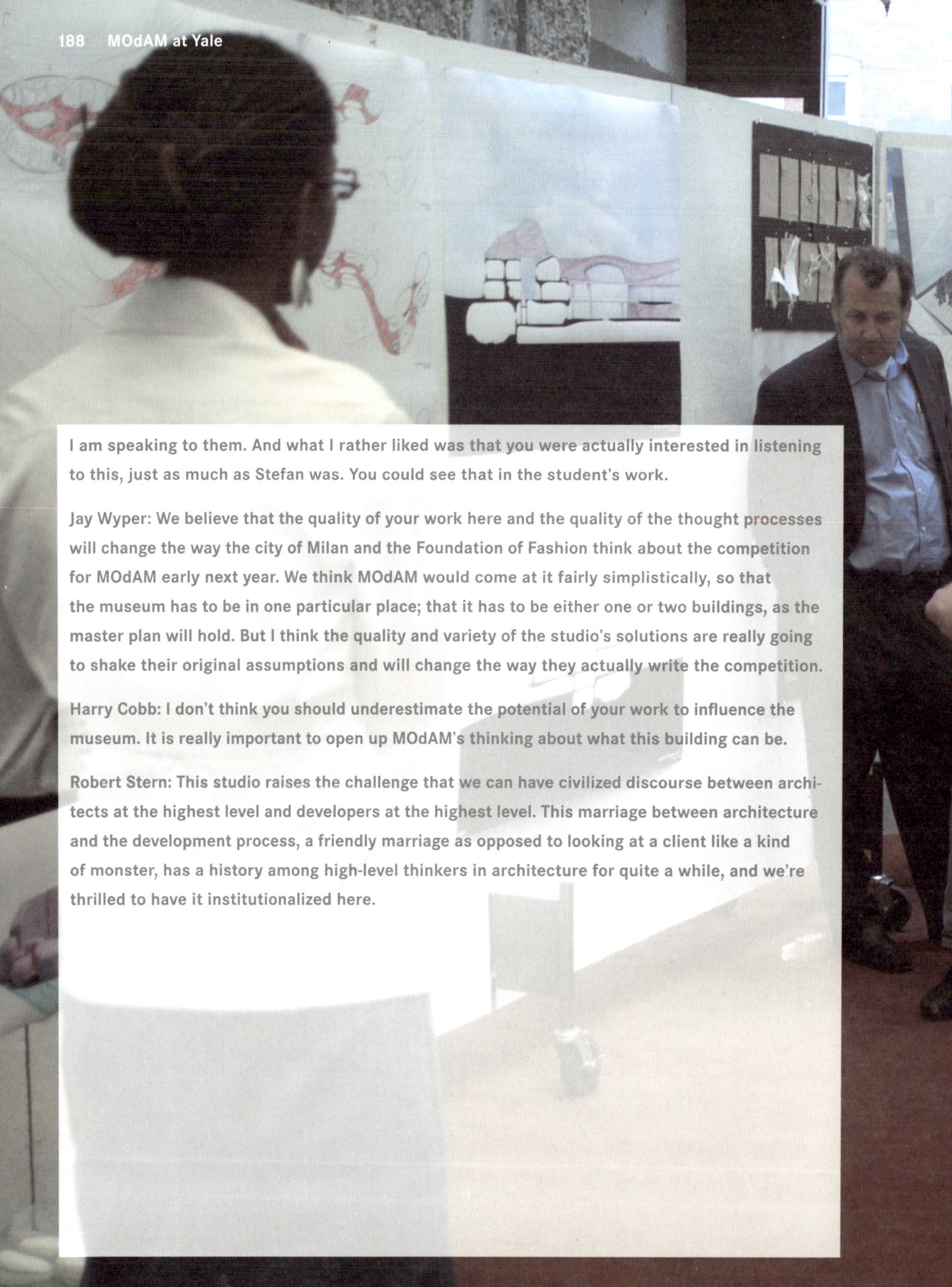

I am speaking to them. And what I rather liked was that you were actually interested in listening to this, just as much as Stefan was. You could see that in the student's work.

Jay Wyper: We believe that the quality of your work here and the quality of the thought processes will change the way the city of Milan and the Foundation of Fashion think about the competition for MOdAM early next year. We think MOdAM would come at it fairly simplistically, so that the museum has to be in one particular place; that it has to be either one or two buildings, as the master plan will hold. But I think the quality and variety of the studio's solutions are really going to shake their original assumptions and will change the way they actually write the competition.

Harry Cobb: I don't think you should underestimate the potential of your work to influence the museum. It is really important to open up MOdAM's thinking about what this building can be.

Robert Stern: This studio raises the challenge that we can have civilized discourse between architects at the highest level and developers at the highest level. This marriage between architecture and the development process, a friendly marriage as opposed to looking at a client like a kind of monster, has a history among high-level thinkers in architecture for quite a while, and we're thrilled to have it institutionalized here.

previous: From left: Cesar Pelli, Robert A. M. Stern, and Henry Cobb.

above: Final review jury, from left: Stefan Behnisch (standing), Tod Williams (seated), Brigitte Shim, Mark Simon (obscured), Cesar Pelli, George Knight, Gerald Hines (obscured), and Jay Wyper.

page 016, Stefan Behnisch, photograph by John Jacobson at Yale School of Architecture, 2005.

page 017, Gerald Hines, courtesy of Hines, 2005.

page 022, Behnisch, Behnisch & Partner, Norddeutsche Landesbank, photograph by Frank Ockert, courtesy of Behnisch, Behnisch & Partner, 2002.

page 023, Ingenhoven Overdiek und Partner, Uptown München, courtesy of Hines (developer), 2004.

page 028, Behnisch, Behnisch & Partner, Norddeutsche Landesbank, photograph by Frank Ockert, courtesy of Behnisch, Behnisch & Partner, 2002.

page 029, Hellmuth, Obata & Kassabaum, The Galleria Houston, Hines (developer), courtesy of Hines, 1970.

page 040–041, Behnisch, Behnisch & Partner, Tsvetnoy Boulevard Project, courtesy of Behnisch, Behnisch & Partner, 2005.

page 042–043, Background image: Robert A. M. Stern Architects and Tusquets, Diaz y Assoc. (master plan architects), Diagonal Mar, Barcelona, Hines (developer), courtesy of Hines, 2002. Graph: Jonah Gamblin and mgmt. design.

page 051, EasyPlan 1.0, Forth Bagley and Jonah Gamblin.

page 052–053, EasyPlan 1.0 Interface, Forth Bagley and Jonah Gamblin.

page 055, Pixel Design Strategy, Garo Balmanoukian and J. Fiona Ragheb.

page 056–057, Garo Balmanoukian and J. Fiona Ragheb.

page 061, Milan 1881, Baedeker-Mairdumont, courtesy of Jonathan Hipkiss.

page 062–063, Braun and Hogenberg map of Milan after a print made ca.1560 by Antonio Lafreri, courtesy of Historic Cities Research Project, http://historic-cities.huji.ac.il, The Hebrew University of Jerusalem, The Jewish National and University Library.

page 065, *Carta delle trasformazioni*, 2005, courtesy of the Urban Center – Comune di Milano.

Carta delle politiche urbanistiche, 2005, courtesy of the Urban Center – Comune di Milano.

page 066, Norman Foster and Partners, Santa Giulia, courtesy of Norman Foster and Partners, 2005.

Daniel Libeskind, Zaha Hadid, Arata Isozaki, and Pier Paolo Maggiora, Fiera Milano, courtesy of Studio Libeskind, 2004.

Massimiliano Fuksas, Nuovo Fiera di Milan, courtesy of Massimiliano Fuksas Architects, 2005.

page 070–073, courtesy of Pelli Clarke Pelli.

page 075, courtesy of Yale School of Architecture.

page 079, courtesy of Stefan Behnisch and Yale School of Architecture.

page 081–085, Pelli Clarke Pelli, Garibaldi Repubblica Master Plan, 2003-2005, Hines (developer), courtesy of Pelli Clarke Pelli.

Page 086, Pierluigi Nicolin, Proposal for the Piazza Garibaldi Repubblica for the City of Milan, 1991.

INSIDE/OUTSIDE, Biblioteca degli Alberi, courtesy of Pelli Clarke Pelli, 2004.

Page 090–091, Hines (developer), Pelli Clarke Pelli (architects), Garibaldi Repubblica Master Plan, 2003-2005, courtesy of Pelli Clarke Pelli.

page 093, Ceren Bingol.

page 094, Ceren Bingol and Jennifer Newsom.

page 095, Genevieve Fu and Brett Spearman.

page 096, Forth Bagley and J. Fiona Ragheb.

page 097, Ceren Bingol and Jonah Gamblin.

page 098–099, Garo Balmanoukian.

page 100–101, Genevieve Fu and Brett Spearman.

page 102–103, Ceren Bingol and Jonah Gamblin.

page 104, Forth Bagley and Jonah Gamblin.

page 105, Benjamin Albertson and Marissa Brown.

page 108–109, Ceren Bingol.

page 110, Forth Bagley and Jonah Gamblin.

page 111–113, Genevieve Fu and Brett Spearman.

page 114–115, Forth Bagley and Jonah Gamblin.

page 116–117, Benjamin Albertson and Marissa Brown.

page 118–119, Ceren Bingol and Jennifer Newsom.

page 120–121, Garo Balmanoukian.

page 122–123, Genevieve Fu and Brett Spearman.

page 126–129, Garo Balmanoukian.

page 130–131, Benjamin Albertson and Marissa Brown.

page 132–133, Ceren Bingol.

page 134–135, Benjamin Albertson and Marissa Brown.

page 138, (top) Ceren Bingol, (bottom) Benjamin Albertson and Marissa Brown.

page 139, Benjamin Albertson and Marissa Brown.

page 140–141, Benjamin Albertson and Marissa Brown.

page 142–146, Ceren Bingol.

page 147, Benjamin Albertson and Marissa Brown.

page 148–151, Forth Bagley and Jonah Gamblin.

page 152–153, Ceren Bingol.

page 154, Courtesy of mgmt. design.

page 155, Haresh Lalvani, Waveknot, computer modeling/rendering, Neil Katz and Mohamad Al-Khayer, 2005.

page 156, Patent application No. 237,503, submitted by S. A. Drewry, February 8, 1881.

page 157, Office for Metropolitan Architecture, Seattle Public Library, courtesy of the Seattle Public Library, 2004.

page 158–159, Courtesy of mgmt. design and Haresh Lalvani.

page 160–161, Benjamin Albertson and Marissa Brown.

page 162, Garo Balmanoukian.

page 163, Forth Bagley and Jonah Gamblin.

page 164–165, Ceren Bingol.

page 166–169, Forth Bagley and Jonah Gamblin.

page 174–176, Ceren Bingol.

page 177, (top) Forth Bagley and Jonah Gamblin, (bottom) Genevieve Fu and Brett Spearman.

page 179–181, Forth Bagley and Jonah Gamblin.

pages 182–189, Review photographs by John Jacobson, Yale School of Architecture, 2005.